I0476384

Day Trading For Beginners

3rd Edition

Day Trading Basics
Do's and Don'ts
And the Small Letters

By

Winston J. Duncan

© Copyright 2015 by Winston J. Duncan
- All rights reserved

This document is geared towards providing exact as well as reliable information in regards to the topic and issue covered. The publication is sold with the idea that the publisher is not required to render accounting, officially permitted, or otherwise, qualified services.

If advice is necessary, legal or professional, a practiced individual in the profession should be ordered. From a Declaration of Principles which was accepted as well as approved equally by a Committee of the American Bar Association as well as a Committee of Publishers as well as Associations. In no way is it legal to reproduce, duplicate, or transmit any part of this document in either electronic means or in printed format. Recording of this publication is strictly prohibited as well as any storage of this document is not allowed unless with written permission from the publisher. All rights reserved.

The information provided herein is stated to be truthful as well as consistent, in that any liability, in terms of inattention or otherwise, by any usage or abuse of any policies, processes, or directions contained within is the solitary as well as utter responsibility of the recipient reader. Under no circumstances will any legal responsibility or blame be held against the publisher for any reparation, damages, or monetary loss due to the information herein, either directly or indirectly. Respective authors own all copyrights not held by the publisher.

The information herein is offered for informational purposes solely, and is universal as so. The presentation of the information is without contract or any type of guarantee assurance.

The trademarks that are used are without any consent, and the publication of the trademark is without permission or backing by the trademark owner.

All trademarks as well as brands within this book are for clarifying purposes only and are the owned by the owners themselves, not affiliated with this document.

Table of Contents

Introduction

Day trading is not a new concept, and has been around since the early 1990's though it is only now that it is becoming really popular with the general population. The simplest way to describe day trading is the practice of trading in stocks on whatever stock exchange within the same trading day. Strictly speaking day traders have to have closed all their positions by the end of the trading day.

Day trading is a high risk business. As a day trader, the chances of you making a loss are much higher than those of someone who trades on the stock market for the long term. As all the money traders make for the day needs to be made in roughly 8 to 12 hours, this can make day trading become a challenge even for seasoned investor.

Though there are many ways to look at day trading, whether you focus on price momentum, trade patterns or a whole host of different strategies, there is one thing that all day traders have in common. They all look for the highest profit margin possible, and for ways to meet their target for the day in the least time possible.

They are able to so adequately because of an understanding of what day trading entails. As a beginner looking to explore this field, it is imperative to understand that day trading is not something you can simply do as a hobby. It requires time, training, patience and understanding. It should be approached as a profession.

If you want to find out what it entails, how to get started, and even understand what you need to set yourself up, then this is the right book for you. This book promises to introduce you to some of the strategies you need to follow to become a successful day trader, the pitfalls you may face, and the successes that you may encounter. It shall also teach you how to make the most of challenging situations when you are trading. So if you are ready to start your journey into the world of day trading, keep on reading. You will not be disappointed.

Chapter 1:
The History of Day Trading

In the beginning of financial trading, the most important US stocks were traded on the New York Stock Exchange or NYSE in a very long and tedious process. After being contacted by a trader, a stock broker would pass on the order to a specialist on the ground who would then have to match the seller's offer with another broker's request to buy shares. Once this match was made, a ticket was drawn up which actually signaled the completion of the transaction.

The commission charged on these transactions at the time was fixed at 1%, meaning that to make any profit on a sale a trader had to make more than 1% on every transaction. Though this may not sound like much, it is a lot when you start piling up the dollars and, for this reason, day trading was not profitable.

In 1975, however, the United States Securities and Exchange Commission (SEC) abolished the fixed deposit allowing for brokers to charge fluctuating interest rates. This was an important move as it was now more lucrative for traders to buy shares while brokers could reduce their commissions, attracting higher investments and, in the long run, making more profit.

This significant change in work ethic had a domino effect on the way traders and brokers did business. On top of the incentives provided by the brokers to entice traders to spend more, this move also meant that the brokers had to reduce their settlement period to fewer days to avoid the larger risks they may encounter.

In any financial trading, the settlement period is the time it takes for any securities that have been purchased to be paid for. In the case of stock market trading, in the past the settlement period could be as long as ten days. These days due to the changes in trade behaviors, day trading included, this settlement period has been shortened to just three days or T+3. This change has also reduced the risk of traders defaulting though this reduction in has also been helped by the advancement of technology.

The Evolution of Modern Day Trading

This technological evolution has been going on for the better part of 60 years, with one of the first and probably biggest advantages of this being Electronic Communication Networks (ECNs). ECNs are primarily large computer-based networks where brokers and traders alike can post their securities or stocks for a certain price (called the 'ask') and other traders and brokers can the offer to buy the stocks at a certain price (called the 'bid').

The first ECN was called 'Instinet' now 'Inet' and it was created in 1969. Its primary mandate was to provide a safe, secure way for major financial institutions to bypass traditional stock exchanges such as the NYSE, making it easier and more convenient to trade insecurities. It also significantly brought down the price of trading and allowed for trade to continue even after the markets had closed for the day.

In the beginning, these ECNs were not geared towards medium and small investors, with some people even calling hostile towards this demographic. This was because they favored large institutions, giving them better prices and, therefore, better returns on investments.

Chapter 2:
Day Trading and the Stock Market

In 1971 the National Association of Securities Dealers (NASD) introduced the first ever fully electronic stock exchange in the world, the National Association of Securities Dealers Automated Quotations more commonly known as NASDAQ. Though it started off as a quotation system, the Nasdaq gained so much popularity that it inspired numerous changes in legislation and practices carried out at the time.

Practices that changed included moving away from paper share certificates, written share registers, use of the postal service, physical shipment and telex to more convenient electronic measures. NASDAQ also pioneered the development of real-time online systems rather than the old batch system.

Probably the biggest change and one that truly benefitted day traders was the changes in legislation that came about because of online trading and registration and the subsequent development of these electronic services. The most beneficial development was the creation of secure, cryptographic algorithms to safeguard the online transactions.

Introducing Market Makers

These changes helped to create 'Market makers' or the equivalent of the NYSE specialists. Market makers are firms that have inventory in stocks from various companies and are in the business of the buying and selling of those stocks online. Market makers sell their stock at a higher price than they would buy the same stock, creating what is referred to as a

'Spread' which is the difference between the asking and bidding figures.

Typically market makers do not care about the value of their shares, just that they sell them off at a higher price than the purchase price. For day traders, these market makers are an invaluable asset as they ensure that there is always an individual or firm willing to buy or sell you shares. At the moment, there are over 500 market makers operating on the NASDAQ.

To date perhaps the most significant impact on the development of day trading was the stock market crash of 1987. This crash opened up the door for the Small Order Execution System or SOES. This system was meant to facilitate low volume trades on NASDAQ meaning that all offers up to 1,000 shares had to be bought or sold immediately, at the sellers asking price. This led to a small group of traders who took advantage of this rule by buying and selling small orders to market makers, making enormous profits in the process.

Electronic Communications Networks and Day Trading

These trades were facilitated by ECNs, and not market makers. In the late 1990's some of these ECNs opened their doors to small investors and traders. Also New ECNs formed, driving competition through the roof and reducing commissions to an all-time low.

This combination of elements opened up the market for individual day traders. The low commissions allow for the individual day trader to purchase higher volumes of stock and make more trades in one day. The market maker in this case makes their money from high volume stocks such as Microsoft and Intel, which have small spreads, therefore allowing the market maker to make huge profits on a rise of just a few cents.

Chapter 3:
Day Trading Basics

As you prepare to plunge into day trading and start reaping profits, there are some basic facts that every new day trader needs to know. By understanding these facts, you will be able to dispel the myths about day trading so that you can operate in a successful manner.

To begin with, here is an explanation of what day trading is not. Day trading is not a high risk method of making money, where you will lose a lot more than you gain, especially in the short run. Neither is day trading a get rich quick scheme, where you can double your capital if it is sizeable enough – especially if you are hoping to do so within a month.

Day trading is often assumed to be simple, with a person sitting in front of their computer and playing with numbers. It is far from simple or easy, in fact, it requires training and strategy to get it right. Finally, day traders are not a bunch of kooky individuals who are their own brand of crazy. A day trader is someone like you, who has identified how to spot and capitalise on an opportunity.

Day Trading and Gambling

For a few years, day trading received a bad rap, particularly because it was being abused. Gamblers, for example, were looking to day trading in order to get their fix. When you consider the odds in gambling and those in day trading, you will be able to see the glaring differences.

In gambling, you are more likely to lose out, especially because the odds are never truly in your favour. With day trading, this is not the case. What is needed instead is proper planning, and one can be successful.

Beware of your Capital

In the process of game trading, you can end up with an unfortunate scenario. That is one where you lose everything, all the capital that you had invested. If you are looking for a way to grow your money and have placed your income into an account for day trading, you have made the wrong decision and could easily end up destitute. What one should do is dedicate some money to day trading, and then forget about it in terms of applicable use.

This does not refer to you using your discretionary income; it actually refers to your risk capital. Risk capital is simply money that you will not mourn over should you lose it. You should be able to afford it being gone.

Day Trading as Business

Should you have made the decision to go into the world of day trading, you need to realise that day trading is a profession or a career choice – it is not something that you do for fun on a Sunday afternoon as you would do with a hobby.

The reason is simple. Day trading requires an investment in time to learn how to get it right, and the development of skills. It also requires a detailed plan, and anyone who is looking to explore day trading as a hobby will likely lack the time to create a plan.

You may get Lucky

As a new trader, you may receive a visit from lady luck and make a significant amount of money from your very first trade. Though this can be fabulous for you, and will definitely build up your confidence, ensure that you continue to work for your future successes. If you are not careful, you may lose all your luck, (and your money) in your next trades.

If you did happen to be lucky, do not take it as a one off. Take the time to analyse and understand what exactly you did to cause such an incredible return. If you can retrace your steps, it makes it easier to apply this strategy to future trades, and hopefully maintain the same momentum.

Choosing a Market

Variety is the spice of life, and when you start day trading, it will appear that you are spoilt for choice. But even spices come with different heat meters, and you need to be careful to pick one that you can stand. This is the same with choosing a market. Here are some of the factors that you should consider.

- Whether you are in good financial health. This has a crucial role to play on the type of market that you will engage in.

- The strength of your personality and your custom trading system. The markets are a tough place to be, and if you do not have a thick skin, you may find that they can easily break you. You need to learn how to pick your battles so that you get closer to success.

- Your location geographically. You may find that you are limited to only a certain number or type of market.

When choosing market, you need to realise that as a newbie, you may be better suited for certain markets, while as an experienced day trader, and you may have enough skill to opt for something a little more risky. Beginning traders should begin by choosing a market that has minimal margin requirements, low tick values and is moving at a medium pace. This will ensure that you are not left hanging with nothing to show for your efforts.

Defining a Hot Tip

When it comes to day trading, there is quite an exchange of information, especially information that is meant to help with profitability. Most traders are privy to hot tips, which promise that if you follow them, you will make a killing. These types of tips are often communicated through the grapevine, and they can best be described as rumours.

The reason that they are so undercover in the way that they are passed on, and even from the person that is providing the information, it that in case of any problems, it is the trader who will be liable.

Should a day trader receive a hot tip which points towards some information that is legitimate, they would have an unfair advantage. This means that other people working in the same area could develop negative relationships or outlooks towards that particular day trader.

Insider Trading

Insider trading is slightly different from getting a hot tip though the way that the information is conveyed to employees is very similar. It is all about finding underground ways to pass the information forward. It is essentially any information that has not been made public, which can be used for the purpose of securing a sale. Insider training will usually be passed forward by a person whose opinion is prominent in a particular field, or who works within the field and has become aware of some new changes.

There are dangers for day traders who act on insider trading tips. These are usually penalties that are imposed should one be found with this information. If you were to profit from the insider trading information, then the penalty would be three times the amount of your profit, and if the government decides that as a trader, you were indulging in criminal behaviour, the penalty could be even higher.

The challenge with insider trading is that it is difficult to prove, as most of it happens with word of mouth, so there is no paper trail. In addition, a lot of the so-called tips that are given out as insider trading, often turn out to be completely baseless.

Chapter 4:
Day Trading Techniques

Day Traders use a multitude of techniques to try and make a profit. Every single one of them is very useful to the average trader though it must be said that flexibility is the most successful strategy a day trader can use. This chapter seeks to outline some of these trading techniques and their relevance to day trading. Some of these techniques involve shorting stocks, instead of buying them, adding an increased risk factor to the transaction. Below are four of the most basic day trading techniques used by day traders everywhere.

1. Trend Following

Trend following is not a strategy used in day trading alone but in all forms of financial trading. It can be defined as the trading in securities and stocks not due to their market value, but due to the particular trends that have been affecting the market values over a set period of time.

In conventional trading circles, the trends can be followed over a period of days or weeks or even months to discern what the best investment would be. With day trading, however, the trend is followed over a much shorter term, a couple of hours at most.

A market 'trend' is the ability for a market price to move over time, whether it moves up or down. Most traders who practice trend following will study the market and wait for a trend to establish itself, and then depending on the nature of the trend, either buy or sell stocks on the market. Trend following is a good way to trade because it allows you the flexibility to decide for yourself whether the investment you are making is sound before diving into it.

Trends are affected by a number of different things, some of which prolong the current trend. For instance, some traders look for information that will confirm their beliefs about a particular trend. Confirmation bias like this has the power to keep the trend going, as once confirmation is found then the investor will apply it to that situation. Therefore, if the trend is negative, the investor will sell his shares to avoid making losses, continuing the negative trend for that particular stock listing.

Factors that have to be considered when trend following include, but are not limited to:

a) **Price:** This is by far the most important thing when it comes to trend following. Though other indicators may be used to forecast price fluctuations, only the actual price will give you an idea of how you need to interact with the market

b) **Risk Control:** Though completely eliminating losses is an impossible task, minimizing your losses should be paramount.

c) **Money Management:** These ties into risk control and are the decision of how much to invest in a trend. Too much and you risk losing more than you should, too little and you may not reap any benefits at all

d) **Rules:** Stick to the rules you laid out for yourself, trend following should be systematic.

e) Diversity: Recent research has shown that diversifying the assets that you follow is vital to professional trend followers.

2. News Playing

News playing is as the name suggests, playing the stock market depending on the news you have received for a particular security or stock on that market. If reports received state that a particular stock is doing well, then that would be a good reason to buy into it. Successful day traders are able to keep their emotions in check while news playing, as they know that emotion should not affect their final decision.

Once a particular news item has been released, it is important as a day trader to look at how this news is affecting the stock prices. As most news will be internally circulated before being released to the public, there may be a slight change in the share price just before any news is released. If there is a negative appreciation of the share price just before a news item is released, then it means that you need to sell your stock to avoid making losses. With day traders, it is said what is perceived is their reality while with conventional traders logic is relied on more.

For instance, when AOL and Time Warner joined forces just before the Dot-com bubble burst in the early 2000s, a day trader's profit margins were very high. Long-term investors at the time were not so lucky, as the merger seemed to have success written all over it, but three years down the road the investment would have proved to be a disaster. In the short term, the perception of the success of the merger was enough almost to guarantee a profit margin for day traders, but with the passage of time that opinion proved to be illogical and hence the losses made by long-term investors

3. Range Trading

Range trading or Range bound trading is a type of trade where a certain asset or stock is watched over a specified period of time. These stocks will have been rising and falling in value in an almost predictable pattern, with maximum and minimum values that can be pinpointed with relative ease and accuracy. The difference between the maximum and minimum values is called the 'range' or 'swing' of the stock value.

Range trading is often thought of in relation to trend following, but that is not the case, as with range trading unless there is an unexpected breakout in the range, the trend remains the same. Once a stock's range has been broken however, it is safe to assume that the trend that broke it be it a breakout (an increase in share price) or a breakdown (a decrease in share price), will continue for some time.

The best way to make money with range trading is to buy the stock when it's on its way back up the channel from its lowest point on the scale, then sell the shares when it reaches its peak. Some range traders even go to the extent of short-selling certain stocks as they know that a higher profit margin will be possible.

Mathematical algorithms in computer programs are often used to eliminate the human emotional factors that may affect a day traders decisions and are often written to give the trader buy and sell signals for selected securities.

Range trading is quite risky for all traders, long term investors and day traders alike, as the risk of making losses increases when trading in a range. A sideways price movement in the share price may also mean that no gains can be made on your investment. Worst of all, if there is an unexpected breakdown in the share prices, losses to you as a day trader can be enormous.

4. Scalping

Scalping is also referred to as spread trading and can be defined as the exploitation of the bid-ask spread by trading in securities rapidly over a very short period of time, usually minutes or even seconds. The theory most traders use when scalping is that if done properly, trading in stocks that make small increments in stock price are easier to catch than big ones.

Most scalpers will make between 10 and a couple of hundred transactions a day in the hope that they will make a profit. Scalpers have been compared to market makers as they help to maintain the liquidity of the market.

There are certain universal principles that all scalpers that trade on the markets are aware of. These are

a) The Lower Your Exposure, The Lower Your Risk

With scalpers holding stocks for just a few minutes on average, their exposure to those stocks is substantially reduced. This diminished time period means that there is a lesser chance of a scalper gaining huge losses due to changes in the stock price.

b) Small moves are easier to obtain

The stock price on any given item is mostly determined by the same old demand and supply principle that drives prices in other industries. In stock trading, this is not usually affected on a day to day basis, but over time. Scalpers, rather than look for big moves with large spreads that rarely occur look for small moves with small spreads that happen more often, increasing their chances of profiting from a sale.

c) Large Volume means Low Profits

Most scalpers will agree that this practice is not suitable for the large capital traders who are looking to move large volumes of shares at one go. This is because the profit margin that is gained from trading in shares with low spread values is negligible to the large investor. For this reason, scalping is more suited to investors who are trying to move smaller volumes more often to gain the biggest profit margins.

d) Spreads are bonuses as well as costs

As most securities exchanges worldwide operate on a bid and ask based system, and then it must be noted that the spreads between these two (the bid and the ask) do become important when you are scalping. When a trade is executed at market prices, it is important to know which side of the fence you are on. If you are the buyer, you will end up incurring costs in terms of the spread, whereas if you are the seller, you make a profit on your sale because of the spread. Sometimes holding on you your shares for a few minutes can increase their value enough that you make significant profits, but not many scalpers are willing to queue (hold on to their shares) preferring to take the small profit margin and repeat the cycle, rather than risk that margin on a 3 minute window that may yield no fruit.

These are just a few of the basic techniques used by day traders and as you can tell all of them come with their own risks and benefits. Traditional long-term investors would avoid some of these strategies as the risks seem too big to take on while the benefits would be minimal. Good day traders, on the other hand, understand that it is for precisely this reason that massive profits can be made, and, therefore, the rewards greatly outweigh the risks.

Chapter 5:
Day Trading Strategies

Now that you have a sound idea of what the best day trading techniques are, you can begin to strategise so that you can make a substantial reward from all of your efforts. The ultimate goal for any day trader is to make a sizeable profit, and in order to fulfil this goal, it is necessary to control a big amount of capital.

Day traders understand that when working towards making this profit, speed and timing is everything. This is because they are focused on finding and making use of the most minute movements in stocks which have a high liquidity or index. Without the right strategy, they are unlikely to success.

A retail day trader can try out the following strategies: -

Strategy for Entry

It is not every stock on the market that is suitable for a day trader. There is a criterion that makes some stock more viable than others. A day trader will evaluate stock based on two variables. The first is the liquidity of the stock. This primarily looks at the pricing of the stock, and the ease with which a trader can enter or exit this stock. The best stock for day trading will have a tight spread, as well as a low spillage.

The second variable that a day trader will evaluate is the volatility of a stock. The mention of volatility explains movement, and in day trading, it refers to the movement in price. When evaluating volatility, the day trader takes into consideration the price range that is expected for the day. This could have two significant results, it could lead to heightened profits or significant losses.

Once liquidity and volatility have been assessed, and the stock has been identified as being appropriate for trading, the next step is to look into the best way to identify entry points.

For this, there are two tools that come in handy.

Candlestick Charts

These charts are highly popular and are essential for any day trader. They display the prices for a specific securities on a daily basis. By analysing a candlestick chart, it is possible to know the day's highest and lowest prices, as well as the opening and closing price.

In addition to this, the shape of the candle in the candlestick chart reveals more information. The section which is wide is referred to as the 'real body'. It is within this section that one can analyse the closing price in relation to the opening price, by assessing whether it was higher or lower. This is denoted by specific colours. When the stock closed at a price that was lower, the candle will be black or red in colour. However, when it closes at a price that was higher, the candle will be white or green in colour.

The shadow of the candle in this chart also tells a story. It explains the highs and lows for the day, and this can then be compared to the opening and closing prices. So in the final analysis, just the shape of the candle will vary based on all the movements taking place in a day's trade. This type of chart provides a straightforward analysis of pricing for the day.

Level II Quotes/ECN

When a gambler goes to the races, they receive a thrill by watching everything unfolding live, right before their eyes. There is an equivalent for this in day trading, and this is referred to as Level II. A trader who is using this strategy is watching the trades being executed live, right before their eyes. This is based on quotes from specific market makers. As everything unfolds, rapid decisions can be made to ensure that any small gain is capitalised on – in real time.

ECN stands for Electronic Communication Network. This is an automated system which allows traders from different locations to trade with each other easily. It works by matching buy and sell orders. This system is great for a day trader who operates as an individual because by using an ECN, the trader can actually connect directly with a major brokerage. This cuts down on fees for a middleman, and also saves time, allowing for faster and more profitable trades. The added advantage of an ECN is that trading extends beyond the typical market hours, and includes after hours trading.

In addition to these two tools, there is a chart that can prove handy when reading information for data trading. Simple being able to understand the information that is available can go a long way in creating a foundation for success.

Discerning the information from day trading transactions would be a challenge if there was no mechanism in place to make it possible. All the information from day trading is arranged in different types of trading charts. By using these trading charts, a day trader is able to keep an eye on the markets that they are trading on, and this makes it easier to make informed decisions about when they should be making their trades. It also allows them to monitor the movements on the market on a consistent basis.

There are a range of different trading charts that are available. These trading charts will all provide you with similar information, and that includes the prices that are currently being traded. Of all the available options, there are three which are referred to with heightened regularity. Candlestick charts have been discussed above. The other two are explained in this section.

Bar Charts

These are basic, easy to read charts that contain all the significant and standard trading information. This information includes but is not limited to the opening prices, closing prices and so on. The layout of the chart makes it very simple to read, and even easier to interpret. There are certain keep bits of information that are also included in the bar chart. The first of these is the open, which is an indication of the first price that was traded during the bar. Next, there is the high, which indicates the highest rice that was trading during the bar. The third piece of information is the low, which gives an idea of the lowest price that was traded during the bar. Finally, there is the close, which details the final price that was traded during the bar.

By reading these prices on the charts, one can make some conclusions about the bar. First, the inclusion of the open and close reveal whether the bar managed to close in a position that was higher than when it opened. Then, the inclusion of the high and low reveal whether the bar fell within a particular range and that range can then be analysed. This range would be the distance that can be seen between the high bar and the low bar.

Line Charts

Of the three types of charts listed here, these are the least popular. When looking at day trading charts as a whole, these are highly popular. In the same way that the other mentioned charts contain all the significant trading information, the same applies to the line charts. However, these charts have the added advantage (or disadvantage depending on your perspective) of only being supported by using charting software.

The charts that are used during trading will all have their own unique way of displaying information, and this means that they also have different ways that they should be read. This in turn will affect how they are interpreted by traders.

There is software available that makes the process of reading these charts much easier for the day trader. This software is also used for creating charts. Almost all day trading brokerages today will use charting software

Defining Stop Losses

The main aim of a trader has been established as making a profit. Day trading is exciting and thrilling. When a day trader is going through the rapid motions of the day, it is quite possible to get caught up in the speed of things and make decisions that may cost money, are reckless or have not been given due consideration.

To stay on the safe side, the trader needs to set up a stop loss order. This will help to guide the sales of the security, as a stop loss order is one where a broker is instructed to make a sale on a security one it has attained a particular price. The aim of putting this in place is to limit the loss that an investor may incur. When an investor is unable to place a significant focus on their daily trading, a stop order comes in handy, as it helps to keep the day's trading within a certain control.

A day trader who trades on margin will be the one most likely to define a stop loss. Once a day trader has determined the amount that they are willing to lose, a physical stop loss order can be put into place. If for any reason a traders entry criteria appears to be violated, then a mental stop loss set at a specific point will be triggered.

All traders need to be careful to ensure that they do not lose everything that they have in their portfolio in a day, simple because they were operating without a clear head or plan. It is imperative that a day traders should set a maximum loss for each day, especially one that will not break the bank. It should also be the type of loss that will not cripple you mentally and financially. No matter what may be happening during the day, when you reach your maximum loss, stop trading. It may be tempting to try and make up any loss in the last trades of the day, but efforts like these in the last minute will usually backfire.

Practice, Perfect, Patch-up

If you are under the impression that the moment you start day trading, having mastered the techniques mentioned earlier, you will make a significant profit, they you are highly mistaken. Have you ever seen a child learning how to get a bike? They get on it, are given a little push and before long, they fall off. They will fall off several times before they finally get it right. The only way that they can develop the skill for riding the bike is through practice.

When you go into day trading, it will be some time before you can make your profit. You will spend some time losing before things begin to pick up. You need to keep practicing the techniques in order to get things right.

Following practice, you can begin to perfect. At this point, you are improving the methodology that you have employed for beating the odds. Patching things up requires an evaluation of a person's personality, to assess whether everyone is on the same page. In day trading, the focus should be on creating a strategy for a good trade, rather than looking at profit as the end all of business.

Chapter 6:
Day Trading Order Types

Whenever anyone is day trading, they need to use orders to complete the trade. Each and every trade will have its own orders, and, therefore, it is vital to understand the different types of orders that exist. Through the use of these orders, a trade can be completed.

Their typical trade will have a minimum of two orders. These would be one buy order and one sell order. One of these orders will be in place for the purpose of meeting the trade, whereas the other will be based on leaving the trade.

They are characterised as single orders, and they work in tandem with each other. Therefore, if you are going into a trade with a buy order, you will have to leave the trade with a sell order.

Following these orders, there are a large number of alternatives that day traders can take advantage of when executing their trades. There are outlined as follows.

Market Orders (MKT)

When it is necessary to buy or sell a contract at the best price that is currently available, this is referred to as a market order. The market is usually quite active, and the result is the price on a market order will change quite a bit. Even though these types of orders are consistently likely to be filled, they are not likely to always be filled at the exact price that the trader was hoping for.

Limit Orders (LMT)

When it is necessary to buy or sell a contract at a price that is specific or has been defined as being a better price, this is referred to as a limit order. When the market is barely moving, then it is unlikely that a limit order will be filled. However, unlike the market order, a limit order will usually be filled at the chosen price. If a better price is available, then it will be filled at the better price.

Stop Orders (STP)

When it is necessary to buy or sell a contract at the best price that is currently available, though they can only be processed once the market has attained a particular price, then this is known as a stop order.

Any day trader will let you know that having a stop order is required. This is because of the risk that is associated with trading and doing business. This in a way helps to offer some protection from the possibility of incurring a big loss. If the order is chosen wisely, and there is sufficient knowledge of the market, then a trader cannot lose.

Stop Limit Orders (STPLMT)

This is a special type of order that combines a limit order and a stop order. This also has special conditions that need to be fulfilled in order for it to be processed. The processing will occur on condition that the market has been able to attain a particular price. This order will then change, and the processing will be done as if it were a limit order. This means that the only time it is possible for this order to he filled is when the chosen price has been attained, or a better price has become available.

Market if Touched Orders (MIT)

This type of order is unique, although it is almost identical to a stop order. What makes it different is that it is only made useful once the market price has been traded beyond the stop price. Also, the trader should be in a position where they only want to order to be processed the moment that the market price reaches the stop price.

Limit if Touched Orders (LIT)

This is another type of order that is also very similar to a stop order. It is different in that it is only utilised once the market price has been able to trade beyond the stop price. The other condition that needs to be fulfilled is that the trader is looking to have the order processed should the market price return to the stop price. It is only in this scenario that the trade can continue and be finalised.

Chapter 7:
The Cost of Day Trading

Day trading can be relatively inexpensive if you use the right strategies when starting out. The right setup can really bring the cost of trading down, especially initial costs. Getting the right equipment is always going to save you some expenses from the onset of your endeavor.

There are also other things to consider such as commission, the type of brokerage firm you are using and the services you shall be engaging in to supply you with real-time market data. Using the standard free market data may seem like a good idea, but keep in mind that this information provided free tends to be delayed and this will not benefit you in any way if you are a day trader. The fact that this data can be delayed by up to 60 minutes means that for a day trader it is extremely unreliable, as even a 5 minute delay can spell disaster for your stock value if it crashes.

This chapter seeks to outline the different strategies that can be used to bring down the costs of day trading by suggesting different cost effective methods that can be used anywhere at any time. These methods have proven to be both cost-effective and productive and have helped day traders in the past realize their full potential.

1. Equipment

Now that you have decided to go into day trading the first and most important piece of equipment you are going to need is a computer and a powerful one. Day trading involves making trades rapidly, and this cannot be done on an effectively slow system.

Market makers right now are using computers that have at least 4 processing cores (like the Intel Core i5 or Core i7) with at least 8 GB RAM. These machines are top of the range and may seem a bit extravagant but as you will soon find out with day trading speed is everything.

They also come with large storage capacities, usually around 500 GB and above. This is needed because the software that you will use and the data that needs to be processed will take up a lot of space in the long term. If you get confused about what kind of machine would be best for you, a good starting point would be to go to an electronics shop that sells a range of different computers and ask for one that is suitable for gaming.

It is recommended that a backup of your system be stored on an entirely different machine, preferably a laptop. This is because when it comes to computers, just like your trading anything can happen. Should any glitches or crashes occur, you want to be able to switch seamlessly to another device to continue trading or at least have your broker's app on your phone to allow you to stay up to date with the market. Another advantage of having your backup on a laptop is so that if you are travelling anywhere, you can stay in touch with the markets via your laptop, as most phone apps will not allow you to have as much control as a full program will.

An array of monitors is also recommended. Two screens are good enough, and four is even better, but the best results have come from systems with six to eight monitors. These give you the ability to see all the information clearly and make quicker, better-informed decisions on the stocks you are trading. The computer and monitor array may seem expensive with the top of the range setups costing about US$ 3,000 and the cheaper options costing US$ 1,700, but for serious day traders, these things are vital as the speed of your transactions is intricately related to the speed of your machine.

The software will also play a significant role, as every serious trader these days uses software to buy and sell securities. When choosing what software to use, it is always important to make sure that the software you are using is widely used, well-known, and relevant when it comes to whatever asset class you are interested in trading in.

The software should also have the following components:

- *Level II* – This is a list of all the buyers and sellers on the market

- *Time And Sales Data* – This is a time-stamped record of all transactions carried out

- *Real Time Streaming Of Quotes And Charts:* A live feed of all market data

- *A Portfolio Tracker:* This will help keep track of your stocks

The software can be very expensive, with some programs being sold at upwards of US$ 5,000. Others charge you per trade or transaction that you carry out. It is important to carry out your own in-depth research to help you choose the right program to fit your needs.

A high-speed internet connection is also important and goes without saying. The most common connection is the Cable Modem Internet Connection though the ideal service to get for trading would be the Fibre Optic Internet Service. Cable internet will supply you with internet speeds of up to 100 Mbps, which is more than fast enough to do basic trading online, but fibre optic internet can provide you with speeds that are ten times as fast. For traders like scalpers who need to have low latency internet, fibre optics is the way to go.

Fibre optic internet is still a relatively new phenomenon, so it is not yet available everywhere, but if it is available in your area it is highly recommended if you want to become a day trader.

2. Brokerage and Commission

Brokerage is an important factor when it comes to day traders as different types of brokers have different ways of doing things and different commission charges.

For instance, market maker brokers though still faster than the traditional brokerage firms are slow to execute trades. For a day trader, the faster the transaction can happen and the lower the commission, the better. Market makers can be slow, especially if they feel more inclined to trade against the order flow for whatever reason. They also charge relatively high commissions for their services bringing down whatever profits you had envisioned making.

On the other hand, discount traders do not share this problem as they charge slight commissions to their clients. The only downside apart from the fact that they are also slow is that they offer very few services and very little support for the client, so a more comprehensive knowledge of the securities exchange market is required if you want to trade through them.

The best option for a day trader when it comes to the brokerage is the direct-access brokers who allow you to trade directly with the ECNs. The result of this is instantaneous feedback from the ECNs and transaction spends that can be measured in fractions of a second. Direct-access brokers are especially useful to scalpers who rely on speed to make the most of their investments.

The average commission rates are about US$ 5 per transaction though on the upper end of the scale commissions of US$ 10 are not uncommon. Unlike retail traders though, direct-access traders charge less commission per unit volume sold. So for instance if the commission on a transaction was US$ 5 for the round trip, a direct-access broker may charge as little as US$ 0.01 per share traded (if more than a stipulated number of shares is traded)

Chapter 8:
Day Trading and Technology

With more and more people venturing into day trading on their own, the use of day trading software has soared in popularity. In fact, many associate day trading with someone who sits in front of their computer all day with numbers moving around and changing.

The use of software can help any day trader increase their profits while also reaching out to traders around the globe. In addition to more individual day traders depending on software, brokerage firms are also taking advantage of software and offering their services over the internet.

The day trading software allows a day trader to carry out all trading activities on their own quickly and efficiently. When a day trader attempts to go through all the necessary processed on their own, they may discover that it is difficult to achieve any type of profit. With an automated software, this becomes considerably easier.

There is one aspect of trading using software that should be taken into consideration. That is making sure that you are using the right software.

Day Trading Software Attributes

Any software that you choose for day trading should have the following attributes.

- The moment that you want to begin trading, the software that you are using should require you to follow a one-step setup process. Through this process, you will put in place some parameters that explain your preferred trading strategy. These parameters include the trading limits that you intent to guide you, ensuring that the system can connect to live data, and allowing it to execute trades on your behalf.

- As you progress in your day trading, you can begin to add even more features to your online trading experience. These include provision for the software to use a stop loss feature.

- Your software should be on an independent platform, preferably one that is web based. This allows you to connect to a site from anywhere, and it also cuts a lot of costs. These costs include maintenance of the software, as well as costs associated with upgrades.

- You should be able to try out a trial version of the software before you make a commitment to use or purchase it. Consider the information that you want to be made available to you as a day trader. You can then set the software to track stocks and give you information on binary options for example.

Setting yourself up

There are certain tools that you need to have to successfully day trade as an individual trader. These are minimum requirements. As you go along and increase in your skills, you will be able to make use of some tools which are more specialised. To begin with, you should have the following: -

- A Computer using the most current operating system available. For now, that would be Windows 8.1. If you are just starting out, a standard computer will work perfectly for you. If you are more advanced and are running your own software, you many need something more specialised. This type of computer would require a very large hard drive. To keep track of everything happening on day trading platforms, you may need to have at least eight screens (monitors) to view.

- o Minimum requirements for your standard PC include a good processor, 2GB Ram, at least 100 GB hard drive, 15" screen size and a network interface (10/100 Mbps).

- High-Speed Internet Access (Day trading is very time bound, so if you have a slow connection, you may be setting yourself up for failure).

- A telephone (You will occasionally need to speak directly with your broker for advice or to give direction).

- Direct Access Brokerage – Allowing you to get your hands on stocks directly without having to go through a middle man,

- Real Time Market Date – Providing you with live information on what is transpiring in day trading markets.

- Day Trading Software – This is software that will provide you information on charting to make it easier for you to track movements.

- Charting Software – You will need this type of software to help you to keep an eye on the markets. This is perhaps the most important software that you can have because it is the one that you shall be using the most. It is able to provide you information on what has happened in the page, and what is happening currently. The results are usually displayed graphically for ease of use.

- A Good Broker – Even though this may not be described as something technology-based, having a good broker is vital towards becoming a successful trader. When you start off as a day trader, you have limited knowledge. On almost all sites, it is necessary to have the details of a broker to ensure that trades can be completed. What is imperative is to search for a broker who will not swamp you with commission fees.

Chapter 9:
Day Trading Mistakes to Avoid

Whenever you are starting any venture, you are likely to lose something or make some mistakes before you get a proper grasp of what you are doing. This is especially true for day trading though with day trading the risks are higher. Here, the risks have to do with money, and this in itself is a challenge. This is because a day trader needs to be quick witted as well as skilful, to be able to purchase stocks and sell them within the same day, and hope that by doing so it is possible to make a profit from the minutest fluctuations in the prices of the stock over 12 hours.

Years ago, day trading was impossible for the average investor, as the tools that were needed were not available to them. These tools included real-time stock results, access to instant traders and the tools for analysis. High-speed internet and Dutch courage have changed this scenario for many who are now willing to try their hand at day trading. There are some things that need to be avoided though, even for the most strong-hearted new trader.

In day trading, making mistakes should be avoided as much as possible because even the slightest mistake can have a massive impact on total income. In order to avoid mistakes, you need to be aware of the mistakes that you could inadvertently make. That is what will be addressed in this section.

Starting Big

As a new day trader, it is likely that you are bubbling with enthusiasm as you look forward to starting your trades. You have read up on all the theory, including the trips and tricks and believe that you are ready for the game. If you have managed a sizeable capital portfolio from an investment, you may be keen to start big, make big profits and please your client.

Even with all the theoretical preparation possible, as a new trader, you need to learn and observe the practical aspects of day trading. With experience, you can take calculated risks.

For this reason, new day traders are advised to start small rather than starting big. This is because when you are likely to make the most significant mistakes in your trading career as you start out. If you have invested in something which has lost you a large amount of money for the client, they you will likely affect your career for the considerable future.

You need to start trading with capital that is minimal so that you can assess your success. After a while, and with your wits intact, you should be able to see successful trading with more than 3 contracts. At this point, you can consider increasing the amount of money that you invest each time, and this should help you get better profits.

Learn the Basics

Day trading is not something that you can simply teach yourself and then start excelling at. You need to get some hands-on advice from people who are seasoned day traders. To do this, you should find an experienced trader and spend some time observing them, asking questions and listening to advice. Learn how to play the game of trading, so that you can build up the confidence to give it a good go yourself. Realise that this will require patience on your part, so that it can be gotten right. With proper determination, you will find that your efforts are enough to lead to big profits.

Planning To Fail

Failing to plan is planning to fail, and this is especially true for day traders. Trading is about making a profit, and not about experiencing feelings of exhilaration by taking chances with money. In light of the outcome that is expected, it is important that all traders have a plan of action.

A plan is particularly important because of the speed and emotion that affects day trading. Day trading are likely to be backed into corners where they need to make instant decisions, or during a volatile day of trading, they could get caught up in the events of the day and make decisions that will negatively affect their bottom line. Have a plan in place, especially when it is in writing, is an important step to controlling day trading.

A day trader, who has taken the time to create a plan which is detailed, will understand what his overall goal will be and will mould behaviour and actions to meet that goal. Within the plan, there should be information on what shall be traded and the markets that the trades will take place in. There will also be details on the methods that will be used for entry and exit into the markets. This will help the day trader avoid buying into a security which would not usually have been considered.

An excellent plan will also have a risk assessment section, with details on the proper reactions to a host of scenarios. This could include how to react adequately to an excellent day of trading, or how to deal with consistent disappointments.

Either way, it is supposed to ensure that the trader remains on track regarding what is required.

Missing Discipline

The best managers, especially those who work in high-risk professions will often create a contingency plan, in case their original plan does not pan out. This means that they are ready for the unexpected.

In day trading, this type of planning is also necessary, particularly because, this activity is highly emotional. Having discipline could be the difference between profit and loss.

An aspect of discipline includes stop-loss orders. These orders are triggered based on certain conditions within the day trading market. They help investors to save money, particularly if the trade is taking place automatically. It is imperative that all traders have a plan that will help them to manage their risks, as well as their possibilities for success or failure.

Manage your Expectations

Day trading is not a get rich quick scheme. Neither is it a magical wand that will help relieve all of your problems. It is challenging, and there is the constant pressure that you could lose it all.

Rather than expecting to rake in the dollars, expect to put in significant amount of work in to perfect the method in which you trade. The reason for this is that success in trading requires a considerable amount of planning, together with hard work.

This planning requires an adequate input of time. Ideally, the time should be well spend observing leaders in the industry so as to discern their techniques.

Being Time Bad

Day trading is already chaotic because of the speed with which transactions are done. However, there is no time that is as busy and chaotic as the first and last 20 minutes of each day. This is because it is the period where investors are the most anxious, looking to make the fastest moves before everyone else appears, or at the end of the day.

As a new trader, this is an excellent example of volatility in the market. It would serve you better to simply wait, rather than join the hubbub. This way, you prevent yourself from making any detrimental mistakes, and you keep away from the competition from institutional traders.

Keeping Too Busy

Being busy is important, and many people want to be observed as being busy, as this is a way that they can validate the amount of work that they have had to do. In trading, being too busy is not good for a trader, it indicates that it is possible to let things slip through their fingers.

A new trader may attempt to manage at least 10 trades in a day. The assumption is by trading more, you can make more. This may not actually be the case. Some professional traders insist on trading just two traders through the day. They may complete the trades early in the day, but then they can spend the rest of the day following up. By having fewer day trades to monitor, it becomes easier to see when there is a change in the market.

If you are a new trader and have achieved success from doing two trades a day, you may be tempted to make more money by increasing the number of investors and trading more. The problem with this is that it may set you back and turn your profitability on its head. This is because you will be stretching your attention. Instead, try increasing the amount that you are trading on your two commodities or for your two investors.

Watch out for Losing Streaks

There is nothing that can be as disheartening as repeatedly losing when you are day trading. If you are not careful, it may reach the point where you end up being clinically depressed, especially if you are always losing more progressively. That is why even though you may have the enthusiasm to day trade on your own, you need to seek out council from a professional who has been successful. Over time, you will pass the phase of losing streaks, and the moments that you were demoralised will be distant memories.

Thinking Anyone Can Do It

Should you ever be in a car accident, and were in need of life-saving surgery, would you allow a teenager in high school to operate on you? Your answer is most likely "Absolutely Not!!"

If you had a large sum of money which you wanted to see grow, would you pass it to the first person that you walk by on the street and say, "I'll wait to hear from you," – highly unlikely.

So when you are looking for a day trader, you need to make sure on certain things, one of which is that the person is qualified when it comes to day trading. They need to have some training as well as possible certification. If you have made the decision to go into day trading without any help, then you also need to ensure that you are capable of making informed decisions. Make sure that you have mastered all the theoretical properties possible and that you have watched an expert practically as well. Remember that you cannot rush the process. It is entirely possible that this could take several months.

Keep an Eye on your Risk Capital

There is every possibility that when you are trading your capital, that you will lose everything. This means that you need to be able to distinguish between your normal capital and your trading capital. Your normal capital includes the money that you need for your day to day living, so that you can pay bills have food to eat, pay your rent or mortgage and have something decent stashed away for your retirement. Your trading capital is money that you are willing to risk. This is money that should be solely dedicated to day trading, and nothing else. That way, it you lose it all, your life will not start to fall apart all around you. It is also noteworthy that a day trader is required to keep a certain amount in their account as equity, and the minimum must be maintained if there is to be any day trading taking place.

Messing up your Margin

Your capital as a day trader is likely to fluctuate up and down throughout the day. Sometimes it is on the lower side, and you need an extra boost. So you choose to borrow from a broker so that you can purchase securities. This is meant to be a facility that gives day traders some wiggle room if it is used correctly. However, some people have used this support in the wrong way or have abused it. This could occur when one borrows much more than they can pay back, and the result is an empty trading account and the mounting of debt. As much as possible, day traders should trade within their means.

Ignoring Important Resources

Perhaps the most important asset that you can get that will lead you to success when day trading online is an excellent high-speed internet connection. Next, is an investment in state of the art software that is specialised and fully loaded with a range of analysis tools. Then you should make sure that your trading wallet is well stocked, as you need a significant amount of capital to get you started. As part of your resources, you should have direct access to an expert in the field so that you can get advice when you need it, and also get input on your equipment and its specifications. Finally, hire yourself a coach. This will be a great investment, allowing you to learn what is necessary to master day trading for the long haul.

Forgetting About Mental Health

Having the right state of mind could be the difference between winning and losing. In order to come out on top as a winner, one who is competent and can trade on instinct, you need to learn how you can manage your emotions. So you cannot allow the intense thinking and mental energy that goes into day trading bring you down and drain your energy. You have to be ready for action, always ready to make a move now. This is like having a jerk reflex. With this as a trick up your sleeve, you will be able to gain competence and win consistently. It will build up your intuition so that you always aim for and attain trading success.

The more that you trade, the better you will become. You need to give yourself the gift of concentration when you being trading. This is so that you can create sweet trading music in your mind. Getting into the zone is something that the most successful traders are able to. It is the trance of trading, and it leads to success.

Chapter 10:
Restrictions to your Day Trading Account

There are several restrictions that are placed on day trading accounts that every beginner should be aware of. Some of these restrictions also have a few regulations ties in to them. The most common are stated and explained in this section.

Requirements on the Margin

The margin account is meant to help tide a trader over during a period of difficulty. If you use a margin account, you could be considered as a pattern day trader. This would be the case if within your margin account over a period of days, you have purchased a security. This is in reference to a rolling five-day period. This period does not include Saturdays and Sundays as well as market holidays.

The consequence of being designated as a pattern day trader is that you need to then maintain $25000 of equity within the margin account, and this is a minimum value. Failure to comply with this will mean that you are not able to do any day trading whatsoever. This is a significant limitation for the day trader that is just starting out. The best thing that a day trader can do to avoid this restriction is to trade within their means and avoid margin accounts.

It may be difficult to do this, especially keeping in mind the advantages of a margin account. What draws in many traders to this option is that a trader can actually leverage an excess of four times of their equity.

Settlements

The speed with which day trading occurs has a significant effect on the way that stocks are settled. Day traders have a three-day period in which they are supposed to settle an official stock transaction following the day the trade was agreed upon. This means that the process of buying and selling will continue to take place, even when the day trader has not been had the chance to clear up and old debts.

However, before a day trader can purchase stock, and then need to have a sufficient amount of money to cover the cost. Some day traders have tried to purchase and sell on the same day so that even if they do not have the money necessary, the profit that they make can cover up the cost. This should not be done. In the worst case scenario, the trader should lean into a margin account.

Chapter 11:
Benefits of Stock Trading

1. It is the best and sure way to get rich

The main way people have of any hope of creating good wealth is through investing in the stock market. This is true in so many ways and it is evident by the increasing number of rich people across the world. If you are keen enough, you will realize that at the majority of people who are newly rich in your area have invested a good amount of money in the stock exchange market. Other investments work really well but with the stock market, you have a high chance of making great returns if you invest wisely.

2. It's the best way to invest other than saving it in a bank

Saving money in a bank is a good way to invest but let's face it; the best investment is one that can give you better returns in the end. A bank's interest is very nominal compared to the amount of money you could get from an investment in a stock market. Some bonds will fetch you good returns in a short period of time if you are lucky and others will give you a considerable amount of money after some time. You get to enjoy great returns while you still have the money that you have already invested.

3. The stock market enjoys a good history

A stock market has a history of going up all the time, and this means that there is a high chance that you will be enjoying good returns from your investments without fail. If you take enough time to study the market first before making an investment, you could be enjoying the best returns than you will ever get in any kind of investment out there. In as much as it is a risky affair, people do not lose all the time, and even though you lose one time, you still get to make so much money in the other investments.

4. The dividends

Some of the stocks you will invest in will pay dividends after every financial year and this means that other than the amount of money you have invested in the stocks, you will be receiving some extra money every time the company makes profits. You end up enjoying a good amount of money in addition to what you have invested in the company. Some companies pay out these dividends on a monthly basis, and if you have enough shares, you get enough money to support you or your family for a long time.

5. Investing in stock market works

If you consider the kind of people that have invested in the stock market, you will realize that they are all acquiring wealth. This should tell you one thing, which is that stock investments always work. As long as you have an effective strategy, you will find it easier to invest wisely, and reap returns quickly.

In the past, the stock market seemed to target the elite in society, but today, it is accessible to everyone. Take the time to learn how the stock market works and you will be enjoying huge returns from it.

6. Market risk is just one risk among many

Stock investing involves a lot of risks; you could lose so much money if you make the wrong investments. But you should know that there are risks everywhere. People who save money in banks risk losing it all as well. People who do not have enough money by the time they retire risk spending all the money before they can stay for some time after retirement. Those people who invest only in less risky investment risk losing their purchasing power to inflation. This means that risks are all over, you just have to choose the best risk of them all; which is a risk that could give you better returns in the end. This makes stock investing a much better option for them all.

7. There is everything for everyone in the stock and bond market

In the stock market, there are stocks that sell at a high price and there are those that cost much less. There are those that guarantee huge returns, and there are others that do not promise any returns at all. We also have stocks from large and well-established companies and organizations, and there are others from companies that are just getting started. The investment choice that you will make will depend on the goals that you have set as well as the risk that you are willing to take. Just remember that those companies that promise huge returns pose great risks and those that do not give hopes of better returns are much less risky. Take time to make a better choice of investment and you will get the kind of returns that you risked for.

8. There are ways to reduce risk in stock investing

Every kind of investment that you will make will involve some bit of risk taking. There is usually no guarantee that your money is safe or that you will get any return on the investment. The good thing about investing in stocks is that you have a choice to the degree of risk that you can take and also, there is a way that you can reduce the risks so as to ensure that you are not losing all the money in case the investment does not go as planned.

Mixing investments is a sure way to reduce the risk of losing your money in stock investments. Consider investing in different kinds of stocks, different companies and in different sectors as well. Plan for it well with the help of your stock broker and/or financial advisor and things may just go well for you. The benefit of this is that you cannot lose in all the investments; if you lose in one, you will gain in the other and so on. By the end of it all, you will still have some of your money, all of it or more.

Chapter 12:
Trading Basics – How to Trade Stocks

Without experience, trading in stocks can be a disaster for your finances because you can lose everything by choosing the wrong stocks. Therefore, you should get a little help so that you can find your feet, and then you can begin to trade in a profitable way. So when you start trading you should: -

Start with a Broker

Once you have your initial investment amount ready, you should hire a qualified and professional broker to begin trading stocks on your behalf. Make sure to learn all the terms and jargon of trading from this broker, so that when you start trading on your own, you understand exactly what you are doing.

An excellent stock broker will be able to explain things to you clearly, and should also be on hand to offer you trading advice whenever the situation should arise.

A broker will offer you three types of services. These include: -

Discretionary Services

These are available for the investors who are only interested in a return on investment, and not on the process of getting that return. The stock broker is given total authority to buy and sell stocks without requiring the approval of the investor. This is excellent in a fast changing market as the broker can quickly react to market changes and then make a profit.

Advisory Services

These kind of services allow for the investor to have greater control of their investment. The broker needs to consult the investor before any decision is made. The broke suggests the best course of action when building up a portfolio, and the investor can then choose what should be done with the investment. Brokers are also available on the phone for consultation.

Execution Services

These are the cheapest support services as they fully depend on the investor and their personal opinion. The broker has a minimal role to play, and that role is simply buying and selling the shares as recommended by the investor. No advice or management of the actual stocks is necessary. This service has increased in popularity over the years as more and more amateur investors increase their skill through using the internet and telephone to do their trading.

Practice Online

There are websites available online that will allow you to practice how to trade stocks before you actually get started. These websites are a good idea if you are working towards eventually being able to trade stocks on your own. Their main advantage is that you will save money as there will be no need to pay a broker.

Web sites will also often have some value added features that make stock trading simpler. These include tutorials, live chats and advice, loans and credit cards.

Using Market Orders and Limit Orders

A market order is a tool that you can use when trading in the stock. What it does is to trade your stock at the best available price at a particular moment in time. It is an excellent way of ensuring an investor gets the most out of a trade. However, its disadvantage is that it has a time lag, and in a rapidly changing market, an investor may receive less than they had anticipated.

A limit order differs slightly from a market order. These orders will create a price window, outside of which, the investors stock will be traded. The advantage of this is that one can enjoy good prices for their stock. However, the disadvantage is that these orders have a special commission that needs to be paid.

Once you have chosen your ideal trading method, you should take note of the stock market opening and closing times. This will determine when you are able to trade successfully in stocks, and also how you can discern stock price displays and stock trading tables.

Reading Stock Price Displays

Understanding how to read stock price displays will make it easier for an investor to discern what is happening as well as to communicate with their broker if need be. Stock prices are quoted using a two-way price methodology. In this methodology, you can see the bid and the offer spread. The bid refers to the price that you are able to sell your stock, whereas the offer refers to the price that you are able to buy your stock. These prices change throughout the period that the market is open during the day.

There is also the width of the spread that should be taken into consideration. This width is affected by how liquid some specific shares are, referring to the ease at which they are traded and the amounts that are traded. Organisations that are trading large amounts of stock will have in place thousands of trades going through at any one time. Their spreads are, therefore, likely to be quite tight.

Reading a Stocks Trading Table

Stock trading tables are found in the pages of financial papers or publications. They usually have 12 columns and a varying number of rows. The stocks that are being traded are indicated in the rows. The columns can be understood as follows: -

a) Column 1 and 2 represent the annual (52 weeks) highs and lows of the stock being traded.

b) Column 3 is where you can identify the organisation trading the stock as it will contain the organisation name as well as the type of stock that is being traded.

c) Column 4 has a symbol known as the ticker symbol, which is a special alphabetical name that is used to identify the stock. Even when trading online, it is important to look for stock quotes from an organisation that has a ticker symbol.

d) Column 5 will indicate the annual dividend pay-out for each share. When no value appears in this column, it simply means the organisation has got to pay out dividends.

e) Column 6 states the percentage return or the dividend, which is the expected yield from the dividend.

f) Column 7 has information on the prices/earnings ratio, which evaluates the latest stock price and the earnings for each share over a period of your quarters.

g) Column 8 indicates the complete number of stocks that were traded on the day. It is important to add two zeros to the number in the column as it is listed in hundreds.

h) Column 9 and 10 show the price ranges that the stock traded in throughout the day, which is the minimum that was paid for the stock, as well as the maximum.

i) Column 11 shows the final trading price recorded for the day by the time the market was closing.

j) Column 12 looks at the net change which is any change in the dollar value of the stock price from the closing price of the previous day.

Chapter 13:
Stock Brokerage Services

Having the money to invest in the stock market is not enough; you need someone to take you through the investment and to advise you where necessary so that you will make the right investment in the end. This is the point where you need the services of a stock broker.

Stock brokers are regulated professionals associated with either a brokerage firm or a broker-dealer. Their responsibility is to buy and sell stocks and other securities for retail as well as institutional clients. They do this through the stock exchange or over the counter for a fee or commission. Stock brokers hold a license, and they deal with particular types of securities and other services. You will, therefore, hire a stock broker depending on the kinds of services you are looking for as well as the types of stocks that you want to invest in.

Importance of a stock broker

- You need guidance in the stock market so as to understand what actually goes on and to make the right choices of stocks to invest in. The right person to give you this kind of guidance is a stock broker. Even if you do your research, you still need practical aid in stock investing, and a stock broker can be of great help with this. You could opt for an individual or an organization of professional stock brokers.

- A professional stock broker is well trained and experienced in the stock market and stock investment. He is the right person to give you the necessary advice you need just before you invest your money in stocks. Investing in stocks is a huge risk to take but with the right information, you can quickly make the right choice of stocks to invest in, which is why you need the help of a professional. Stock brokers have been in the market for an extended period, and so they can tell the trends in the stock market.

- Buying and selling of stocks cannot be done entirely by you; you will always need a representative to carry out the sale and purchase with your best interest at heart. It is much easier for a licensed professional stock broker to complete the transactions for you. Alone, you may not accomplish anything – you could even make a loss. Therefore, a stockbroker is a critical person in these kinds of investments.

What stock brokers do is to open an account in their company or firm in your name, and then manage it for you. The account is the same as the one you open with a bank but the difference is that it will not have financial information, but information pertaining to the stocks that you have invested in.

Finding the right stock broker

Finding the right stock broker is the best financial decision that you will ever make. A lot of people who succeed in the stock market have the best stock brokers working for them. This is the bit you need to take very seriously in order not to waste your money in the investment.

- Determine the objectives of your investment

If you are investing a large sum of your money in stocks, what you need is a stock broker that has the best capabilities in going for stocks with the best returns in the market. If you are investing a small amount of money, you will care so much about the cost of his services and the fee structure. The kind of a stock broker, you will go for will be determined largely by what you want to get out of the stock market. Note that those stock brokers who charge so much money as commission are not always the best at what they do; there are affordable stock brokers who deliver great results all the time.

- Choose whether to trade or to invest

You have two options in the stock market, either to trade or to invest for the future returns. Trading involves buying stocks and selling them as soon as there is a good chance to do so; that is after an increase in the price of the stocks. Traders aim to get small and recurrent profits, and they buy stocks several times and sell them the same way. Investing, on the other hand, involves lending out your money to a certain company or companies for a suitable period of time and then getting good returns out of it.

If you are investing, you need a full-service stock broker. He will be analyzing the stock markets for you and advising you on the right company to invest in. If on the other hand you are wanting to trade, you may consider a discount stock broker in order to save money on their commissions so as to maximize the returns that you get after every trade.

- Find out just how much help you will need from a stock broker

The kinds of services you need from a stock broker will be extensively determined by the kind of stockbroker you will be going for. If for instance you are new in stock investing, you need advice, guidance and you have so much to learn from a stock broker, so a full-service stock broker will be the right one to hire. If on the other hand you want to do a lot of things by yourself, maybe you have already studied what needs to be learned about stock investing and you feel that you can do this on your own, just set up an account with a discount stock broker. It is always good to determine what you want first so as to hire the right stock broker.

- Determine the kinds of stocks you want to invest your money in

Different stock brokers deal with different kinds of stocks. Therefore, you will hire a stock broker depending on the kinds of stocks you want to buy. Some brokers only deal with mainstream companies, and so you will need another stock broker if you decide to invest in low market capitalization companies.

You can go to a stock broker that deals with all kinds of stocks if you unsure of the kinds of stocks that you really want to go for in the beginning. Better still, make up your mind about the kinds of stocks you will invest in first, and then hire the best stock broker to take you through the investment.

- Make sure that you are dealing with an insured and licensed stock broker

Fake stock brokers will definitely disappear with your money, which is why a license is important when you are hiring a stock broker. Ensure that the stock broker is registered with Securities Investor Protection Corporation as well so that you will not lose any money to any kind of risk. You have to ensure that your account is insured at all times to minimize the risks of losing all your investments. If you are lucky, you will get a stock broker that carries an extra insurance from a private insurance provider, which is great for you. This is, in fact, the first thing you have to be sure about before you can start talking to a stock broker.

Factors to consider when hiring a stock broker

With the above considerations, you will definitely end up with more than one stock broker that you have to compare. At the end of your comparison, you should hire just one, who will provide all the services and help that you will need as you get started in stock trading. Below are some factors that will make choosing the right one easy:

i) The cost

Stock brokers differ in the way that they charge for their services. If he is offering the kinds of services that you are looking for, and he is a well reputable broker, you will go to the one that charges the least amount of money so as to maximize the returns that you get out of your investment. Some stock brokers charge commissions plus other charges, so you have to consider all these charges before settling to one stock broker.

ii)   Stock broker capabilities

Expert stock brokers can advise you on the right kinds of investments to go for so as to ensure that you are not losing any money in the end. If you want a stock broker that will be responsible for buying and selling your stocks, it is best to go for the most capable because he will always make the right decisions for your gain. Check out the past record of the stock broker and you will be able to choose the best one to deal with.

iii)   Trust

This is very important since the stock broker will be managing your account and all the money that your stocks will be generating. Licensed stock brokers can be trusted. You can also get a referral from someone that is currently using a trustworthy stock broker so as to be at ease even as you trust him with your investments. It is always good to conduct a background check on the stockbroker you are interested in so that you will be sure that he is trustworthy and quite reputable.

iv)   The company or firm he represents

Many stock brokers work for a certain brokerage company and so, you have to check out more about this company before you can hire their services. Ensure that the company is reputable, with a good track record of performance and very capable to manage your investments. So many people are investing in stocks these days so it will be so easy to get the information you need about a certain brokerage company or firm.

v)   The kinds of services they offer

When hiring any kinds of services, it is always good to determine how the service provider serves his clients. Choose a stock broker that will give you quality support services every time that you need them. Some stockbrokers are known to treat their clients unprofessionally, or to be unavailable at odd hours, which is not something you would go for. Ensure that they have the best customer support services so that you will always be treated as a valuable customer.

Types of stock broker fees

Both the full-service and discount stockbrokers charge a certain fee for their services to their clients as discussed here:

a) Commissions: this is the fee charged by the stockbroker who executes your buying and selling of stocks. This fee is charged per transaction that the stockbroker executes. Discount stockbrokers charge a relatively lower commission when compared to a full-service stockbroker. Always compare the commissions charged by different stock brokers before you can proceed to work with them to be sure that you are not paying more money than you should.

b) Asset based management fees: stock brokers will charge you a certain percentage of your total assets that are under their management instead of charging commissions of the same. Their annual fees do not usually go beyond 2%, so it is usually not a huge amount of money although this depends on the stockbroker you are dealing with.

c) Premier account: premier accounts are offered by stockbrokers to the investors that want to enjoy more services from their stock investment accounts. If you upgrade to this kind of account, you will be charged an amount of money but you will be able to enjoy credit cards, checking accounts and other great services depending on the stockbroker that you are dealing with.

d) IRA custodial fees: you will be charged for any IRA related paperwork that your stockbroker will do for you. Even though some stockbrokers waiver such fees, they end up charging their clients on a yearly basis.

e) Inactivity fees: this is the fees charged for those investors that have been unable to generate a certain amount of fees or commissions as per their agreement with the stockbroker. This means that you have to be active throughout to avoid paying this fee.

Trading in Stocks without the Help of Stock Brokers

As discussed in this chapter, the role of a stock broker is very paramount when it comes to stock investing. Stock brokers are supposed to make work easier for investors and the stock market is designed in such a manner that it can be really hard for an investor to do it himself, although this does not mean that it is impossible. If, for instance, you are the kind of investor that does not trade frequently, you may want to save some money and decide to sell your stocks directly without the help of a stock broker.

Selling your stocks directly will involve a much longer process, and this means that it will take more time than if a stock broker was helping you with the sale. Another thing to note is that you will not have control over the stock price. This means that you could sell your stocks at a much lower price that you could have anticipated.

These days, investment firms allow investors to trade in their stocks directly without necessarily involving a stockbroker. The role of a stockbroker in the modern day stock market is slowly diminishing as many people look for ways to minimize the expenses and maximize the returns.

Different ways to do this are:

- ✓ Contact the transfer agent of the company whose shares you want to sell and see if he can be of help to you. If he agrees, you will send your shares directly to him. In this case, you will be required to sign the stock certificates and hand them over to him, and then you will agree on the cost of the stocks, and the deal will be sealed. Some transfer agents will charge a small fee for this but most of them offer such services for free, so if you are lucky, you will not be charged a dime. The recent average share price will be used to determine the cost of the stocks that you are selling.

- ✓ Direct purchase plans will not require you to have a stockbroker as well. Many corporations usually buy and sell their shares through direct purchase plans or through dividend reinvestment, and this is a sure way to trade in stocks on your own. The plan will always keep your stocks in the account and it allows reinvestments of your dividends in order to increase the number of shares you own in that company. If you want to sell your shares, you can contact the plan administrator for an easier trading. The cost of stocks, in this case, will be determined by the recent average share price.

✓ You are allowed to sell your shares directly to your friends or relatives without necessarily involving a stockbroker. What you need for this transaction are your stock certificates. The buyer will only need to have money or a certified check. Just endorse the shares to the buyer and sign on them. You may want to check out other requirements that the company's transfer agent will need so that you will seal the deal without wasting so much time on it.

✓ Set up an online brokerage account and take full control of your buying and selling of stocks. The internet has brought so many changes in the stock market, and this is just one of them. What you need to find on the internet is an online trading company. These days, there are so many online trading companies that will allow you to set up an account and start trading in stocks. If you have studied stock investing in detail and you are sure that you can do it, this is the way to go so you will not have to deal with a stockbroker ever again.

If on the other hand you are a frequent trader in the stock market and you would want to invest more money in more stocks, it is always good to have a stock broker as his services could come in handy when you need any kind of help with your investments.

Chapter 14:
Stock Trading Strategies

Now that you have understood the trading basics, you can begin to come up with a strategy to trade your stock. There is a two-pronged approach to stock trading strategies and those are looking at short term movement where it is possible to earn profit on the price changes from a stock, or long-term strategy, which entails buying the stock and then holding on to it for a long period of time.

Short term movements occur in a strategy known as active trading. In active trading, the investors are under the impression that they can make significant profits by monitoring the short term movements and taking steps to capture the market trend.

The long-term strategy is also referred to as a buy and hold strategy and the reasoning behind it is that the price movements that occur over a long period of time will be more profitable than the price movement that occurs over a short period of time.

Investors who are interested in making money quickly through stock trading will go for the active strategies when trading stocks. There are various types of active trading and buy and hold strategies. These techniques are explained in this chapter.

Day Trading

This is the most common method of trading used by investors practicing active trading. It is the way in which stocks are traded during the day. In this type of trading, at the end of each day the positions are closed out. There are no position that are held open overnight. Whereas in the past, only specialist brokers used this method of trading, today more upcoming investors can use this method thanks to being able to trade online.

Swing trading

This is the type of trading that occurs when there is some price volatility. It occurs when a trend breaks, which is usually at the end of a trend, right before a new trend is able to establish itself. The swing trade is held for a shorter time than the trend trade, although they often help for more than a day.

Scalping

Scalpers try to make profits on the stock market by making a large number of small moves in a short amount of time. It is a quick strategy for getting a return. It works by taking advantage of the different price gaps that occur as a result of bid/ask spreads and order flows. This is a low-risk strategy because scalpers try to hold their position for very limited periods of time.

In addition to these strategies, there are certain techniques that you need to understand and possibly master.

Breakouts

This is a common technique used when trading. It requires identifying an excellent price level and then trading while the price breaks an earlier determined level. The logic behind this technique is that if the price is able to get enough force to move beyond the earlier determined level, it will continue to do so. Breakout trading helps an investor take advantage of upward trends in the market. It also centres on the concept of support and resistance.

What all investors hope for during the breakout period is that the prices of the stock will continue to increase until they actually surpass their all-time high. In order to make the most of a breakout, a broker can place a limit order which will allow a trade to occur automatically once the price moves to above an expected high or below low.

In order to avoid experiencing losses, breakouts should not be done during a period where the market is not trending. The reason is because false trades may occur which could result in losses. Losses occur because of a loss of momentum in the market.

Momentum Trading

This is a technique that is used when an investor or broker is working with the force and continuation of precise entries of stocks. The broker expects the price of the stock to move towards the direction of a particular trend, rather than expecting there to be a break out at a particular place. This type of trading works for a person who is good at planning because it requires an analysis of the indicators that affect stock prices, which include moving averages or oscillators.

If the stock being traded appears to be able to benefit from a long term strategy, then momentum trading can easily come into play.

Retracements

This technique requires some skill on the part of the trader. The trader needs to be able to identify clearly which direction a price should move in and maintain confidence that the price will continue to move in that direction. The reasoning behind this drinking is that following each move in a particular direction, the price is likely to move in reverse direction temporarily as the traders capitalise and take their profits.

In this period, the amateur investors will try to trade in the other direction. These moves are known as retracement or pull backs. The same concept of support and resistance is used with retracements just as it is with breakouts.

This type of trading is only carried out when the stock market has been affected by economic events or news that shocks the market. It is generally deemed to be ineffective if one is looking to make a proper and sizeable return.

Position Trading

This is a technique that is used for traders who are aiming for long term trading. It uses information from all the other strategies and techniques to come up with a trend for the current condition in the market. Then a trade takes place. This trade is not completed immediately; it may take from several days to several weeks to be finalised. This is because if depends on the trend.

What happens with trend traders is that they try to benefit as much as possible from trends that are moving up or down in the market. Trend traders will ensure they get into the trend once it has had the opportunity to establish itself. Once the trend begins to break, the traders will immediately exit their position.

The main purpose of traders in position trading is to make sure that they are in the market when the prices start to make a move. The type of asset one has should be taken into consideration when attempting position trading. This is because the trader needs to have confidence that they are able to hold their positions for as long as the trend lasts for them. This will entail them being able to discern and take advantage of other people's emotions when they are liquidating their positions and taking profit in the wake of a short term trend, over their long term trend.

Chapter 15:
Stock Trading Tips

As you become more stable and confident in your stock trading, you can take advantage of a few tips to keep you making a profit and the right moves. Here are some tips which will help you remain profitable.

Tip 1 – Purchase and hold stocks instead of rushing into trading

In the past, the costs of trading were quite high as brokers charged high commissions to finalise a trade. Today, commissions are distinctly low which may mean that it makes more sense to trade more and more frequently. This would be a wrong assumption. Even though commission costs are lower, there are a range of other costs that have come into play. There include markups, which are placed by brokers, as well as higher taxes being imposed on short-term trades.

When trading in the short term, active trading, more attention should be given to the price fluctuations of the stocks. An investor who is unable to pay close, continuous attention to the stock market may find that they miss out on profitable scenarios, and then they could lose a large amount of money.

Tip 2 – Diversify your Portfolio

The different industries in the market could be affected by a myriad of factors. Should one industry see, the significant upheaval of any nature, investors in that industry could lose out big time. That is why it is important to hold stocks from a range of different industries. This will allow you always to have something to fall back on in case of an issue with the economy and one industry.

Tip 3 – Carefully select your trading style

This tip applies to investors or traders who opt to trade online because usually they do so without the added support of a broker. You should be able to determine the pros and cons of your trading strategy, and whether you are interested in something short term or long term. The decision of how you would like to go about trading should be made before you actively start to trade.

Tip 4 – Start off with a low-risk method

There is nothing as disheartening as losing a significant amount of money on the stock market. If you are just starting out, a big loss could even mark the end of your stock trading days. Therefore, as you begin, give yourself some time to learn how to trade by selecting low-risk stocks. In addition, take some time to learn about risks management so that you can trade online successfully.

Tip 5 – Selling is just as important as buying

There is an emphasis that is placed on buying stocks, especially in choosing the right stock for a sound investment. However, selling of stocks is equally as important as buying stock. Do not neglect to sell your stock and allow yourself to lose out on stock gains. Your stocks will only give you a profit once they are converted into cash, and not by resting in your portfolio.

This requires you to plan ahead and set the criteria that you will refer to so as to determine when the right time to sell your stocks is.

Tip 6 – Avoid chasing 'hot tips'.

This is surely a term that you have heard before in reference to stocks. A hot tip usually indicates a stock that is giving high returns at the moment, or apparently attracting a large number of investors because of a short term return that is highly likely. Even though everyone may be rushing towards this investment, it is important for you to do some research, and clearly understand their reasons for doing so. You may as well be gambling if you make an investment decision based on a little bit of information that often cases, cannot be verified.

Tip 7 – Have a long term perspective

Trading in stocks should not be your get rich quick strategy. Therefore, avoid being tempted by the promise of short-term profits once you begin trading. The investors who get the best returns are those that are in it for the long haul. Therefore, you should be patient once you start trading and take your time so that you can make a more significant return.

Another reason that a long term perspective is preferable likes in the amount of time that people have to invest in trading. For someone looking to try active trading, they must make sure that they have the time, education, finances and most importantly, the drive to make sure that they are successful.

Tip 8 – Sell your losing stocks

The stock market is not stagnant, and it can move up or down without any warning. An investor interested in making a profit is highly likely to sell their stocks when their prices are higher. However, what often happens with declining stock is that the investor will hand on to it in the hope that there will be some sort of rebound in the market, and the stock will then appreciate in value.

Rather than keep the stock until it sinks to the point of being worthless, declining stocks should be sold so that at least some return is gained.

Tip 9 – The afternoon is the best time to trade

Whether you are located on the east coast or the west coast, you should be able to trade without concern for major changes in the stock market. The afternoon is, therefore, the best time for you to trade. This is because across the country, any important information that could affect trading has already been discussed. Even though it may seem like a good idea to make a trade at the beginning of the day, you should take some time to evaluate the pattern that the stock market is taking through the course of the day. In this way, you can tap into a profit or avoid losses.

Tip 10 -A new investor should always be ready to take some small losses.

Stock market investments pose a great risk if you are not careful, and so you should always be prepared for the worst. Though this may seem negative, it only means that you can truly celebrate when you get a good return. This is the only way you can invest with minimal or no stress. This is also the same reason why you should start investing small and not place all your money in one investment. Experts always advise investors to risk an amount of money that they are willing to lose.

Tip 11 – Do not be discouraged

Persistence is required when you are learning to invest in the stock market. Some traders lose hope along the way, and they do not get to enjoy returns from their investments. If you want to succeed in stock trading, you have to be patient and learn bit by bit. Remember that most rich people across the world have earned their wealth this way, so you should learn patience in order to enjoy great rewards in the future. Take your stock trading moment by moment, and then day by day.

Tip 12 – Concentrate on a few, high-quality stocks

In as much as it is necessary to spread the risk by investing your money in more than one company, it is good to note that the quality of stocks matter in stock investing. There are stocks that are well known to be of great quality, and these can guarantee good returns in the future. These are the ones you should be investing in. Financial advisors could be of great help in choosing the right stocks to invest in. Your stock broker can also help you choose great quality stocks to invest in. Do not invest in just any stock.

Look at a company's earnings, the earnings growth, profit margins, sales, return on equity and so many other things so as to determine the quality of that company's stocks. This will help you make the right choice of a company to invest in.

Tip 13 – Choose your sector wisely

The best sectors to invest in are for instance entertainment and leisure, computers, software, communications technology, drugs and medical sectors and specialty retail. These are the leading sectors you should be eyeing if you want to start stock trading. They have strong sales and earnings, and their stocks are always trending.

Tip 14 – Do not expect to buy low and sell high

High expectations during stock trading may discourage you if things do not go your way. The last thing you need at this time is pressure to sell high, as not all stocks follow this pattern. These days, investors are encouraged to buy high and sell even higher. Stocks that are doing well in the stock exchange market will not come cheaply to you; you have to pay more to gain even more. New investors should therefore not be made to believe that they can sell high if they buy low. This is an easier way to get you to buy stocks that will not give you the expected returns.

Tip 15 – History always repeats itself in the stock market

It is important for a new investor to read widely about the past performance of stocks they are interested in so that they can make the right decision. If the stocks at one time did very well in the stock market, there is a probability that they will do the same in the near future and this marks a good investment option. If on the other hand a certain stock you are interested in has a history of failing investors, do not be duped to investing in it.

Chapter 16:
Buying and Selling Stocks Online

Technological advancement has made things much easier for investors such that they no longer have to go through a stock broker in order to buy or sell their stocks. These days, discount stock brokerage companies and firms are offering online accounts and access to trading for investors that want to do it on their own.

In order to enjoy this convenience, you need to choose an online brokerage firm to deal with and open an account with them. These online firms have made buying and selling of stocks so easy such that new investors can easily do it with minimal or no hassle.

The only challenge in this is that you will need to develop your own investing strategy that will produce good returns for your investment portfolio.

Getting started with buying and selling stocks online

- You need an online broker. There are so many online brokers these days, and so you should vet them carefully so that you make a good choice. It is always advised not to base your broker selection only on the commissions they are charging, as there are other more important things to consider. These are for instance your investment goals, broker's trading tools, products offerings, their customer services and then the commissions and other fees that they charge. Taking your time to make a selection will definitely give you a good stock broker to work with. Compare different well rated online brokers and choose the one that offers exactly what you are looking for.

- Choose the kind of account you need to open with the online brokerage company. There are mainly three kinds of accounts offered by brokers, and these are cash, margin and retirement accounts.

  o A cash account is meant for an investor that wants to start stock investing with a small amount of money or plan and to buy and hold share investments.

  o A margin account, on the other hand, is meant for investors that would want to borrow a portion of the cost of stocks bought.

  o The retirement account are for tax qualified investment retirement accounts.

You will choose an account depending on the goals that you have set for your investment as well as the needs you have for that investment.

  - Now that you know the kind of account you need, and you already have a broker to work with, fill in the broker's account application. Since this is an online application, this can be done through your broker's website. You will be required to come up with a username and a password for that account. Once the registration is complete, and the account is approved, you can login to your account and get started.

  - You need to fund your account. Read through the broker's website for payment details that you can use in order to send money to your account. In most cases, the brokers offer more than one way through which their clients can send money to their accounts. Choose a means that is more convenient for you and that which will take less time and not charge a lot of money.

- Take the time to learn the trading tools provided by your broker as these will be of great help to you once you start stock trading. You need to know how to look up the prices of stocks for instance, how to find the current value for your investments, and the tools you will use in order to buy or sell stocks. Learn as much as you can and ask so many questions through the customer support so that you will be able to manage your account by yourself with no problems at all.

- It is important for you to learn about the different types of stock market orders. Find out when you can use each of these types. Your online brokerage account's trading screen provides you with a chance to enter many types of stock market orders which may include stop orders, limit orders and market orders. You are able to control how long a certain order will be left open. These are important details to learn about as they will help you a lot when you start trading.

- Once all this is done, start searching the stocks to invest in. Most of these online trading sites provide research tools that can give you access to the kinds of stocks that you could be interested in. Study them carefully before you make the choice of stocks to buy. Study each stock as well as the company that is selling the stocks and use your wisdom to make a good choice. If you make an informed decision, you will reduce your chances of losing your money in an investment.

Benefits of buying and selling stocks online

A lot of investors have abandoned the traditional way of buying and selling stocks with the help of stock brokers, and they are now buying and selling stocks online. This means that there are a lot of benefits they enjoy from this electronic trading as discussed here:

a) Online stock trading services are very easy to access

With just a click of a button, you are able to access these services as long as you are connected to the internet. Any investor is able to access these services with ease. If you have access to the internet, you will also need money in a checking account for the investments. A stock trading account can be set up quite fast and then you can transfer the funds directly from your account. Once this is done, you can start trading with ease.

b) The cost of transactions is much lower with online stock trading

Business people will always be advised to go for a business chance that will reduce the cost for them because this always means that more profits are realized in the end. This is the reason why online stock trading is much better because you do not need to pay commissions and other fees as it is required if you are dealing with a traditional stock broker. Professional stockbrokers are well trained and experienced, and so you have to pay a lot of money for their services. Online stock trading services are automated, which reduces the cost of placing trades and this is how you end up paying less transaction fees.

c) Online stock trading allows you to manage your own investments

The reason why people deal with stockbrokers is in order for the stockbrokers to manage their investment accounts. This happens mostly in case the investor does not know a lot about investing in stocks. As a result, the investor ends up paying huge amounts of money to the stockbroker as commissions and other fees, and this reduces by a huge percentage the profits the investor gets from the investments.

Online stock trading services, on the other hand, allows the investor to manage their own investment accounts. You are able to buy and sell stocks freely as you please without necessarily asking for the consent of anyone. You can make your own decisions and enjoy a higher profit margin from your investment once you start trading online.

d) Online stock trading is more convenient

The internet offers convenience services all through as long as you are connected. This is true even for online stock trading. You can trade from anywhere as long as you can access your online stock trading account. This is much better than dealing with a stock broker. If you want to buy or sell stocks, you can do it much faster than if you were dealing with a broker. These online stock trading accounts are accessible any time of day and so, you can always check out your investments with so much convenience as often as you want.

e) Subscription fees for online stock trading accounts are manageable

There are subscription levels offered for different kinds of investors. The amount of money they pay is not a lot; it is much lower when compared to how much money you would pay if you were dealing with a stockbroker. There are accounts that you can operate for free and only pay some money after every trade. Other accounts are charged on a monthly basis, but investors operating these accounts are allowed to trade for a much lower fee. You are provided with all these options before you open up an account so that you will choose an account wisely.

Chapter 17:
Common Stock Investing Mistakes You Should Avoid

Making mistakes in stock investing is always a part of the learning process because, as an investor, you will do your best to avoid committing the same mistake. However, mistakes in investing are used to differentiate between a great investor from a poor one. Just know that all investors have made one mistake or another while they were investing, so if you make one mistake or two, it should not be the end of your desire to invest in stocks.

Mistakes in investing could make you lose a huge amount of money, which is a risk that investors should not always be willing to take. That is why it is great to learn about some of the mistakes that you could make as an investor, which you can easily avoid for successful investing.

1. Going for stocks that appear cheap

The belief many investors hold off buying low and selling high does not hold at all. Many investors end up losing so much money to cheap stocks. If the prices of the stocks that you want to buy have fallen, there is a good reason why that is so. Do not assume that the price has fallen in order to allow investors to buy and hope that the price will shoot up in no time.

Always take the time to determine why the stock price has gone so low all of a sudden. The company might be in serious problems, meaning that the stock price will not go up anytime soon, and this means that you will have to wait for a long time to enjoy some benefits.

What if the stock price continues to go down? It will be a huge loss on your part, so always be wary of stocks that appear to be cheap.

2. Using margin excessively

Margin is the amount of money an investor borrows as a loan in order to invest in stocks. This is just a loan and so, in case your investment does not go as planned, you will end up paying huge debts without any profits to enjoy. This is the reason why margin should be used sparingly during stock investing.

Many investors look at the margin as free money and so, they invest in just about any stock that they feel will give them some returns. This is dangerous investing because just the same way you will not use your own hard earned money to invest that way, you should not use the loan money to do the same. After all, you will be paying this money back with huge interests.

As a new investor, use margin wisely if you have to use it. Financial advisors advise new investors to avoid margin by all means but in some situations, it is necessary. Understand first all its aspects and dangers before you can invest using margin and you will be careful to use that money wisely.

3. Taking Part in Day Trading

This is a dangerous game that a serious investor should not take part in especially if you want to become an active investor. Day trading is done by those expert traders who can risk losing large amounts of money. Besides, you need specialised equipment for this, so if you are a new investor, it will be hard for you to access the equipment and to afford the amount of money required for day trading.

Day trading requires the expertise, the equipment and fast order execution that you may lack if you are a new investor. It is advisable for you to take the time to study the market, build your wealth bit by bit before you can think of day trading.

4. Underestimating your investment abilities

There are so many successful stock investors these days, but this does not mean that they are the only ones meant to succeed in such investments. Many new investors think that they have to give way to the prominent investors and that there is no chance for them to do so well. This is what limits your abilities to invest and enjoy huge returns in the end.

Do not underestimate your potential in the stock market or your ability to make huge profits. Remember that if you acquire the right trading skills and you are willing to take more risks, you will be as successful as those investors that you have always admired. The stock market provides an equal chance for every kind of investor, even if you do not have so much money to invest, therefore, go for your luck.

5. Averaging down when compounding your losses

Investors should always know that they can make mistakes when investing, which is just human. If you make a mistake and you end up losing money, the best thing to do is to accept it and face the reality after all other investors make mistakes, and they lose money too. Acting fast enough will save you so many losses in the future, and it is the right thing to do.

If for instance there are changes in the stock price that you bought, first of all, determine the reason why the stock price went down. If there is no chance that the stock price will go up anytime soon, accept the loss and move your money in another company that has a good promise. Act as fast as possible and you will never have to worry about losses you encounter along the way.

Smart investors do this all the time, and they have come to realize that losing and gaining is part of stock investing, therefore, do not beat yourself up if you get into a loss. Holding onto a company that does not promise anything good in the future will make things much worse for you, therefore accept the mistake fast enough and move on.

6. Overlooking the big picture when buying a stock

Qualitative analysis of a company you want to invest in will be of great help to you before you make that investment. Always look at how successful the company is and how that success will be in the near future before you can invest your money in it. If the company is able to move with the changing times, for instance, it is safe to invest in it. But if the advancement in technology will affect its growth and success, this is not a company to invest in.

Accessing the company qualitatively is as important as checking out its sales and earnings. These are the most important factors that will determine if the company is a good one to invest in or not. A company dealing with ordinary mobile phones, for instance, will not stand the time with the smart phones flooding the market. Investing in such a company will not be a good idea so it would be best to look for another alternative as fast as you can.

7. Do not pay too much attention to others

Irrational decisions do not end up well for stock investors, and these come about when you listen more to what other people have to say about stock investing and rushing to change the belief you previously had. There are all kinds of advice that will come up as well, and you have to be careful not to change your trading strategy without carefully thinking about it.

Many investors fall because they keep changing their strategies but if you are able to determine your trading strategy and sticking to it all the way, you will end up growing your investment portfolio.

Always trust your actions and decisions and in case you want to change anything, take the time to study about it. This way, you will not risk your investment portfolio in any way.

Conclusion

Now that you have been introduced to some of the basics of day trading, you can begin to understand the avenues that are available to you when it comes to trading on the stock market.

The steps outlined in this book are just the beginning, and to become a successful day trader you will need to do more than just study the markets and start picking up little nuances like different trends and how they affect stock prices.

There are many websites online that offer you the chance to try your hand at day trading on a simulator BEFORE you even start trading on a real market, and such websites are going to have to become an integral part of your study as you explore this field of trade.

Normal investors call day traders gamblers for a reason, and that is because every day really is a gamble. Good day traders have been known to make over US$ 150,000 a year, but that does not mean they did not have their bad days where they lost a few thousand in the wrong security.

Remember, good discipline, and good money management are key to being a good day trader. Also, not allowing your emotions to run away with you when it is time to make a trade, or when you have heard some news is also imperative. Try as hard as possible to be logical and thorough when it comes to your trading practices, and with time even you could be making a 6 figure salary from the comfort of your home.

*****Free Bonus*****

To get your free report <u>click here</u>:

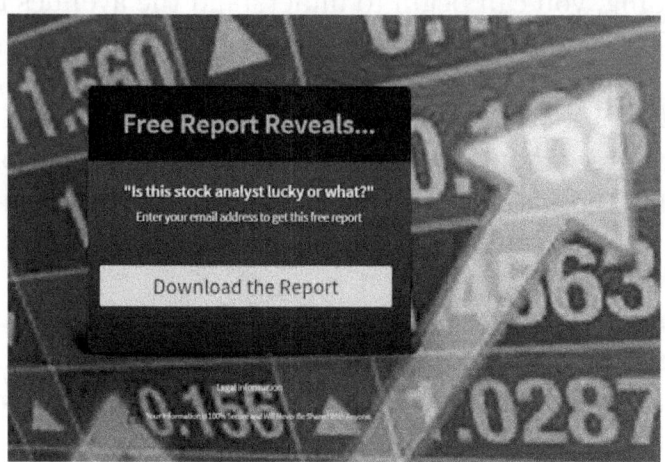

*****Free Bonus No.2*****

STOCK TRADING FOR BEGINNERS

Stock Trading
Basics and Strategies

Table of Contents

Chapter One:
Introduction to Stocks and Options

In order to understand options, you must first understand stocks as they are interlinked but different. Being a business owner without having to show up at work using stocks and options takes some understanding of both, and without that understanding, you could end up losing a lot of money and wasting a lot of time.

The dream of being a business owner who doesn't have to leave home and still make a lot of money is not a pipe dream. Stocks are the cornerstone of any investment portfolio. Having a solid understanding of this piece of the puzzle is a must.

If you take a look at the time over the last few decades, you can see that the interest in the stock market has grown greatly. The stock market used to be a toy for the rich to play a game, but now it's a way to grow your wealth and make a lot of money. This demand joined with advances in the trading technology has created a way for markets to allow almost anyone to own stocks and options.

Unfortunately, while they are popular, most people don't really understand stocks. A lot is learned from their friends, peers, and family rather than actually talking to a stock broker or even picking up a book about stocks and options. But you don't have to be that person. You chose to pick up this book and educate yourself about this topic.

Most of what you will hear from family and friends pertains to people *losing* money in the stock market rather than *making* it. Be aware that this sensationalism comes from the misinformation of get rich quick schemes and scams. Stocks are not the magic answer to wealth, but they can make you wealthy if you know what you're doing. Stocks will create massive amounts of wealth, maybe for you, but they do not come without risk. Understanding the stock market and where you're putting your money is going to make you a lot better at making money.

Now, an investor's portfolio usually includes items such as stocks, bonds, and mutual funds, but there is a fourth option at their disposal! These are known as options. Options are versatile, and that's where their power lies. They allow the trader to adapt or adjust their position according to a number of situations that might come about. Options are able to be speculative or conservative. You can do just about anything from protecting a position or declining or outright betting on the movement of the index or market.

However, the versatility of options is not without cost. They are complex and can be riskier than a stock. That's why you'll see plenty of disclaimers telling you that options trading is very risky and should only be done with risk capital.

If someone tells you that options' trading does not come with risks, then they are not to be trusted. Even if you know what you're doing, you can still lose a substantial amount of money, so be careful. Due to this risk, many will suggest that you forget they exist and steer away from them, but being ignorant of another type of investment option will put you in a weak position.

Even if you do not decide to invest in options, you ought to understand them so that you know what is happening if someone makes an offer to you. Not learning how they function is just as dangerous as investing in them without being educated about them, so I urge you to read forward even if you are not willing to take the risks.

Most multi-national, multi-million dollar companies offer options to employees and others so you may want to pay attention.

Before we discuss options, I am going to go into stocks in case you're completely new to the stock market world. Even if you're not, you may want to continue reading in case you learn something new.

Chapter Two:
What are Stocks

In short, a stock is a share in the ownership of a company, but they are really much more than this. They represent a claim to the company's earnings, as well as assets. When you acquire more stock, you acquire a greater part of the company's ownership. Stocks are also known as equity and shares, so be aware that when someone uses those terms they are really talking about stocks.

When you hold a company's stocks, you are a shareholder or a partial owner of the company, and that means you have a claim to everything the company owns. Usually, this is a small claim. So technically, you own a sliver of every piece of furniture, trademark, and contact the company has. As an owner, you will get some of the company's earnings and will be able to have voting rights if they are attached to the stock.

Stocks are represented by certificates, which are fancy pieces of paper that prove you are a partial owner. You usually won't see these documents during our modern times because they are recorded electronically, and this is known as holding shares in street name. This is done so that they are easier to trade. In the past, when you wanted to sell a share, you had to physically take the certificate down to the brokerage office. Now, all you have to do is click a link on a website or make a phone call. Life is much easier for everyone involved.

When you're a shareholder in a public company, it doesn't mean that you have a say in the daily operations of the business. Instead, you can vote once per share in order to elect a board of directors at annual meetings, and that's the extent of your say in the company. For instance, if you're a shareholder in Microsoft, you don't get to call up Bill Gates and tell him that you think the company should create a program or change a program. In the same line of thinking, if you're the shareholder of a beer company, you don't get to just walk in grab a free case of beer.

The management of the company is going to increase the value of the company for the shareholders. If that doesn't happen, the shareholders can vote to remove the management in theory. In reality, an individual investor like you or me would not own enough shares in order to have a material influence on the company. It's the really large investors that have the say-so in a company.

For an ordinary shareholder, not being able to have a say-so in the managing of the company is not that big of a deal. After all, the idea is to not have to work to make the money. The importance of being someone who holds shares is that you're entitled to part of the company's profits and you have a claim on the assets. Profits can be paid on the forms of dividends. The more shares you have, the larger your portion of the profits is. Your claim on the assets is only relevant if the company goes under. In the case of liquidation, you will get what is left over after the creditors are paid.

Another important part of the stock is its limited liability. That means that as an owner of a stock, you're not liable if the company cannot pay its debt. Other companies that are set up as partnerships are set up so that if the company goes bankrupt, the other partner or shareholder can be liable to the creditors. They can come after you personally and sell off your car, house, furniture, and other worldly possessions in order to get the debt that is owed to the company. Owning a stock means that the maximum you can lose is the value of the investment. Even if a company goes bankrupt, you will never lose personal assets.

Debt versus Equity

So why does a company issue stock? Why would the founders want to share the profits with thousands when they could keep it all to themselves?

The reason is that, at some point, most companies need to raise money. In order to do this, they can borrow from someone or they can sell part of their company, which is issuing stocks. A company can borrow by obtaining a loan from a bank, or they can issue bonds. Both methods are under the umbrella of debt financing.

On one hand, issuing a stock is known as equity financing. Distributing stock is good for the company because it doesn't require that the company pay back any money they borrowed or make payments on interest as they go. All they have to do is pay out dividends when the stock declares they will. The first sale of stocks is known as the initial public offering or IPO.

You may not think that it's important you understand the difference between a company that finances through debt and finances through equity, but you would be in the wrong if you did. When you purchase a debt investment like a bond, you are assured the return of the principal amount you paid as well as assured interest payments. This isn't the situation with equity investment.

When you become an owner, you undertake the risk of the company not making it, just like a small business owner is not guaranteed to be successful. As an owner, your claim to the assets is less than the claim of the creditors. This means that if the company goes under and liquidates their assets, you will not be able to touch any of it until the creditors have been paid first. This is known as absolute priority. Shareholders can earn a lot if the company is successful, but they can also lose a lot if the company is not.

Risk

I believe I would be amiss if I did not emphasize that there is not a guarantee when you purchase an individual stock. Some companies are going to pay out dividends, but others are not. And there is not an obligation to pay out dividends even if a company has traditionally done so. Without dividends, an investor can only make money through the appreciation of the stock on the open market. On the downside, a stock that goes bankrupt leaves the stockholder with nothing.

While the risk might sound very negative and turn you away from the stock market altogether, there is a bright side. Taking on a greater risk will demand a greater return on investment. That is why stocks have outperformed other investment options like bonds and savings accounts. Over the long-term, an investment stock has an average return of around ten to twelve percent.

Now that you're aware of the risk involved with stocks let's talk about the different types.

Chapter Three:
Types of Stocks

There are two different types of stocks, common and preferred. Depending on how much you're investing, you will have the choice between the two.

Common

Common is the one that is usually referred to during pleasant conversation. Common stock is most of what a company puts out when they issue stock. They represent a share in the company and a claim to dividends or a portion of the profits. Investors of this type of stock get one vote per share when electing a board member, who will oversee the major decisions that are made by management and the company.

Over the long term, common stock yields a higher return than almost any other investment when it comes to capital growth. This higher return can come at a higher cost because common stocks have the most risk. If a company goes bankrupt, you will not receive anything until the creditors are paid. In addition, you won't receive anything until the preferred shareholders are compensated.

Preferred

A preferred stock is going to come with the same degree of ownership in the company, but it's not going to come with the same voting rights. With a preferred share, an investor is going to guarantee a fixed dividend forever. This is unlike a common stock because a common stock has a variable dividend that is never guaranteed. Another advantage is that if liquidation occurs, a preferred shareholder is going to be paid before a common one. However, a preferred shareholder will still only be paid after the creditors are paid. Preferred stock can also be callable, which means the company has the option to purchase back the stock from the shareholder at a premium.

Some consider a preferred stock to be more representative of a debt than equity. A good way to think of a share like this is to think of it like a share that is between a bond and a common share.

Classes of Stock

While the common and preferred stocks are the two main forms, it's also possible for a company to customize their different classes of stock however they want. The most common reason to do this is because the company wants the voting power to remain with a certain group. If this is the case, the company will give different voting rights to different shares. For example, one class could be held by a select group who are given ten votes a share rather than just one.

When there's more than one class, the classes are designated Class A and Class B. The different forms can be represented by an a or b being placed behind the ticker symbol of the stock, such as BRKa or BRKb.

Companies can create many different classes of stocks, so be aware of what you're looking at and always do the research on the company's website.

Chapter Four:
Trading Stocks

When you go to purchase a stock or trade a stock, you're most likely going to go to an exchange, which a place where a buyer and seller meet in order to decide on a price. Some are physical locations and transactions are carried out on the actual trading floor. You've most likely seen some photographs of trading floors, where the traders are throwing their arms in the air, waving, yelling, and signalling. It really is a wild ride. There is another type of exchange, though. This is a virtual exchange that is made up of a network of computers where traders discuss and trade electronically.

The purpose of a stock market is to enable the exchange of stocks or securities between the buyers and sellers, which reduces the risk of investing. Just imagine how difficult it would be if you had to call around yourself in order to sell your stock. Really, the stock market is nothing more than a sophisticated market place where buyers and sellers are linked together.

Before I move on, I should tell you the difference between the primary and secondary market. The primary market is where the company will sell their IPO's or securities, and in the secondary market, investors will trade or sell a previously-issued security without the issuing company being involved. The secondary market is usually what most are referring to when they say 'stock market.' It's imperative to understand that the trading of a company's stock is not going to involve the company at all.

There are two famous stock markets in the United States, the New York Stock Exchange, and NASDAQ.

The New York Stock Exchange

This is the most prestigious of stock markets across the globe and goes by NYSE. It was founded over two hundred years ago in 1792 when the Buttonwood Agreement was signed by twenty-four New York City stockbrokers and merchants. Currently, this stock market is the market of choice in America due to its big name company players.

It's the first type of exchange where most of the trading is done face to face on the floor. This is also denoted to as a listed exchange. Orders will come in through a brokerage firm where members of the exchange are located and it will flow down to the floor brokers who will go to the specific spot where the stock trading is taking place. At this location, which is also known as the trading post, there is a person who is known as a specialist whose job is to match up the buyers and sellers.

The prices are set using the auction method. The current price is the highest amount the buyer is willing to pay and the lowest price where someone is willing to sell. Once the trade is completed, the details are sent to the brokerage firm, who will notify the investor who put in the order. While there is human contact in the process, computers still play a huge role in the process.

The NASDAQ

This is the second type of exchange and it's a virtual type called over the counter or OTC market. The NASDAQ is the most popular of this type. An OTC market does not have a central location or a floor broker. The trading takes place through computers and telecommunications with a network of dealers. In history, the largest companies listed with the NYSE while the other second place companies would trade on other exchanges. However, the tech boom of the late 1990's changed all of this. Now the NASDAQ is home to many big companies like Cisco, Microsoft, Dell, Intel, and Oracle. Therefore, NASDAQ is a serious competitor of NYSE.

The NASDAQ brokerages seem to behave as market makers for different stocks. A market maker is something that provides a continuous bid and ask price in a set percentage spread for shares. They can match up buyers and sellers directly, but they usually maintain an inventory of shares in order to meet the demands of investors.

Other Exchanges

The next largest exchange is the American Stock Exchange in the United States, also known as AMEX. AMEX used to be an alternative to NYSE, but that role is now filled by NASDAQ. NASD, the National Association of Securities Dealers, is the parent of NASDAQ. NASD bought AMEX in 1998. Therefore, now almost all of the trading is small-cap stocks and derivatives.

There are numerous stock exchanges that are located in almost every country across the globe. American markets are the largest, but they are still just a fraction of the investment opportunities across the globe. The other two financial hubs are London and Hong Kong, home of the London Stock Exchange and the Hong Kong Stock Exchange respectively.

The final place that's worth a mention is the OTCBB or Over The Counter Bulletin Board. This term refers to companies that are too small to meet the listing requirements of a regulated market, including the NASDAQ. The OTCBB is the home of the penny stocks because there is almost no regulation. This makes investing in the OTCBB market riskier than most.

Now that you're aware of how stocks are traded let's look at the different causes of drops and rises in prices.

Chapter Five:
Causes of Stock Prices Dropping and Rising

The stock prices are always fluctuating on a daily basis due to different market forces. Market forces are the supply and demand of the stocks. If more potential shareholders want to purchase a stock than sell it, then the price will go up. At the same time, if more people would want to sell the stock rather than buy it, there is a greater supply than demand, and the price falls.

Understanding supply and demand is pretty simple. What is difficult to understand is what makes people want one stock over another. This can come down to figuring out what news is positive for companies and what is negative. There are numerous answers to this complication, and just about any investor is going to have their own strategies and ideas.

With that being said, the main theory is that the price fluctuation of a stock indicates what the investors feel the company is worth. Do not think that a company's value is only in the stock price. The value of the company is the market capitalization, which is the stock price times the number of shares that are outstanding. For example, let's say a company trades at $200 per share and has 3 million shares outstanding, and has a lesser value than a company that trades at $100 that has 6 million shares outstanding. Two hundred dollars multiplied by three million shares is six hundred million dollars. One hundred dollars multiplied by six million shares is six hundred million dollars. Therefore, they are pretty equal.

To further make things more difficult, the price of the stock is not only reflective of the company's current value, but also the growth that investors want to see in the future. The most important factor that is part of the company's value is its earnings. Earnings are the profit the company makes, and a company cannot survive the long run without them. It makes sense if you think about it. If a company doesn't make money, it isn't going to stay in business. Public companies are required to report their earnings quarterly. Wall Street pays rapt attention to these during the earnings seasons. The reason is that an analyst will base the future value of the company on the earnings projection. If a company's results are greater, the price jumps up. If the results are disappointing, then the price falls.

However, it's not just earnings that will change the sentiment toward a stock. It would be pretty easy if that were the case! During the dot-com era, dozens of internet companies capitalized in billions of dollars without actually making a profit. As most of you know, the valuations of the companies did not hold and the internet businesses saw their values contract to just a fraction of their peak. Still, the fact that the prices moved demonstrates that there are factors other than the current earnings that influence the stock market.

Investors developed hundreds of ratios, variables, and indicators. Many of you may have already heard of the price/earnings ratio, or the Chaikin oscillator.

So why do the prices change for stocks? The best answer is that no one really knows. Some believe it's not possible to predict how a stock will change while some believe that making a chart and looking at the past price movements will tell them. The only thing that is certain is that stocks are always changing.

The important things you should have gathered are:

- That at the most basic level, supply and demand in the stock market is going to determine the stock price.

- Price multiplied by the number of shares outstanding is the value of the company. Comparing just the share price of two companies is not going give you good, valid information.

- Earnings should be what affect an investor's value report of a company, but there are other indicators that they use in order to predict a stock price. Remember, it's the investors who ultimately affect the price of stocks.

- There are numerous theories that attempt to explain the way the stock prices move and why they do, but there is not any one theory that has a good explanation.

Now that you know how the stock market prices fluctuate let's look at how to purchase stocks.

Chapter Six:
Buying Stocks

You now know what a stock is and some about the principles behind the market they're traded in, but how do you actually purchase a stock? Fortunately, a trip to the stock market in New York City is not in your near future unless you really want it to be. There are two main ways to purchase stocks.

Brokerage

Using a brokerage is the most common way to purchase stocks. They come in two different styles. Full-service brokerages will offer you expert advice and will manage your accounts, but they do charge a hefty price. Discount brokerages will offer very little personal attention to your portfolio, but they are cheaper.

It used to be that only the wealthy were able to afford brokers because they were expensive and full-service only. When the internet came about, the explosion of online discount brokers also made an appearance. Thanks to the internet, almost anyone can afford to invest in the market.

DIPs and DRIPs

DRIPs are dividend reinvestment plans and DIPs are direct investment plans. These plans are how individual companies, at a low cost, allow a shareholder to purchase stock directly from them. DRIPs are an excellent way to invest a small amount into a company at a regular interval.

Purchasing stocks is not difficult at all. All you have to do is go online and sign up on a reputable website in order to start trading.

Conclusion

I hope you found it informative and insightful about the world of stocks trading.

Proper research of the market and making the right moves will let you reap huge profits from options trading. It is not so complicated, which you must have figured out after reading this book.

I hope that this eBook was informative and engaging enough for you to give options trading a thought.

Enough Theory - Practice makes perfect. Happy Trading.

www.ingramcontent.com/pod-product-compliance
Lightning Source LLC
Chambersburg PA
CBHW070816180526
45168CB00002B/633